Speak Up and Stand Out

Speak Up and Stand Out

How to Make Effective Presentations

Nanci McGraw

SkillPath Publications
Mission, KS

©1997 by SkillPath Publications, a division of The Graceland College Center for Professional Development and Lifelong Learning, Inc., 6900 Squibb Road, Mission, Kansas 66202. All rights reserved. No part of this publication may be reproduced, stored in a retrieval system, or transmitted in any form by any means, electronic, mechanical, photocopying, recording, or otherwise, without the written prior permission of SkillPath Publications.

Project Editor: Kelly Scanlon

Editor: Jane Doyle Guthrie

Page Layout: Rod Hankins and Premila Malik Borchardt

Cover Design: Rod Hankins

Library of Congress Catalog Card Number: 97-66334

ISBN: 1-57294-070-0

10 9 8 7 6 5 4 3 2 1   97 98 99 00 01

Printed in the United States of America

Contents

Preface vii
Acknowledgments ix

1   Facing the Fear 1
2   Assessing Your Readiness for Success 15
3   Recognizing the Importance of Image 23
4   Polishing the Sounds of Successful Speaking 29
5   Tapping the Power of Body Language 43
6   Identifying Your Objectives 51
7   Anticipating Your Audience 59
8   Writing Your Speech 73
9   Choosing Audiovisual Aids 91
10   Creating Your Environment 111
11   Handling Special Speaking Opportunities 123
12   Welcoming Feedback 133

Checklists: The Master Plan 143
Bibliography and Suggested Reading 151

Preface

If you're completely alone, talking out loud to yourself, then I guess that's "private speaking." The minute you speak to another person, that's "public speaking." There's a message and a purpose that you're conveying with words, voice, and body. We usually just call this kind of public speaking "talking," and it doesn't seem scary. But somehow when we formalize it at all, by increasing the number of people within the sound of our voice, the size of the room, or the importance of the occasion, "Anxiety" (with a capital A) arrives.

I wrote this book for those who want to meet public speaking anxiety and put it in its lowercase proper place. I won't diminish the work ahead, or trivialize the task, but it's doable.

Speak Up and Stand Out: How to Make Effective Presentations is dedicated to anyone who attempts the difficult, and to all who desire to rise above mediocrity.

Acknowledgments

When I was in the fourth grade, my teacher wrote on my report card, "Nanci is a little radio. Now if I can just figure out how to turn her off!" Thank you to that teacher and many others over the years, who identified a communication skill that brought me to this place. However, talking and public speaking are not the same. When you finally figure that out, your public speaking progress is ensured.

Thank you to the many role models who demonstrate the positive power of language and the elevated skill of complete communication, even oration—trainers, teachers, professional speakers, news commentators, talk show hosts, politicians, activists, salespeople, religious leaders, and certain impassioned people with a message. Many stand up, but not all stand out for positive reasons. The ones who do stand out are in fact outstanding, and have my respect and gratitude.

one

Facing the Fear

Q. Why should I force myself to do something scary?

A. Because it's good for you.

That's not all. Good communication skills are a prime "power broker" in our personal and professional lives. The ability to shine when you speak in front of groups can (at the very least) move you ahead and (at the very best) literally catapult you to a level of success you never dreamed of. Here are six reasons (out of the many you might identify) why you should commit to polishing your presentation skills:

- Develops courage, poise, and self-confidence in a quick, effective way
- Enhances your self-image and propels you forward in business, civic, and community activities (or any area where you want to exert influence)
- Expands recognition from people you think count, because you're noticed for positive reasons
- Increases your chances of getting promoted (you're viewed as an asset to the organization)
- Accentuates your leadership skills; the higher up you go, the greater your need for fine-tuned public-speaking skills
- Intensifies your ability to inspire others

As Daniel Webster summed it up, "If all my possessions were taken from me with one exception, I would choose to keep the power of speech, for with it, I would soon regain all the rest."

Obviously, the case is easily made. But there's still that one big hurdle: fear. The *Book of Lists* shares the top fears people have in life, and speaking before a group is number one, while fear of death comes in at number seven! Evidently (according to repeated surveys) public speaking is more devastating than bankruptcy, more anxiety-provoking than divorce. Why?

If you've ever felt the sting of disapproval or rejection to any degree when you've spoken in public, then even the *anticipation* of repeating that activity, even the slightest *possibility* of recreating those negative emotions, produces *fear*. And since it's probably more likely that you'll have to speak in front of others than face snakes or bankruptcy, public speaking pops up as a major concern and activity to avoid!

Public speaking by definition places a person in front of others, on display, on parade, taking center stage. Though some people from a very early age seem to seek the spotlight and thrive on performing, telling jokes, or being the center of attention, most of us are very selective about how much of that we really want, and in what circumstances. When all eyes turn to us, most of us feel the pressure to be at our best, because negative response cuts at the very core of our self-image (what we know about ourselves) and self-esteem (how we feel about ourselves).

No matter how experienced, no matter how lofty the position, virtually every person faced with public speaking experiences *some* form of stage fright. Stop right now and face that fear by completing the following exercise.

Facing the Fear

4

Exercise
•••••••••••••••••••••••
Identifying Symptoms of Stage Fright

Look over the following list and check off those symptoms of stage fright that affect you:

- [x] Shaking knees
- [ ] Trembling voice
- [x] Fidgeting hands
- [ ] Breathlessness
- [ ] Coughing or constricted throat
- [x] Dry mouth
- [ ] Flushed face
- [ ] Ashen appearance
- [ ] Self-consciousness and physical awkwardness
- [x] Frequent need to go to the restroom
- [x] Queasy stomach
- [x] Excessive perspiration
- [ ] Sense of time thrown out of whack (time speeds up or slows down)
- [x] Forgetting your train of thought
- [ ] Forgetting where you are
- [ ] Forgetting who you are

Speak Up and Stand Out

That'll do for starters . . .

The bad news is, you're normal. However, the good news too is, you're normal.

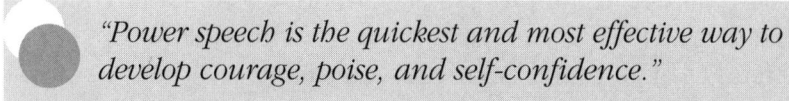

> "Power speech is the quickest and most effective way to develop courage, poise, and self-confidence."
>
> —Roy Alexander, *Power Speech*

> "When it comes to public speaking, many are called, but few want to get up."
>
> —Anonymous

Facing the Fear

Decide to Tackle the Challenge

Fear of speaking shouldn't stop you from becoming an outstanding public speaker. Consider the following:

- Winston Churchill fainted from fright during his second speech before the House of Commons.
- Stage-side observers of Mario Cuomo during his keynote address to the 1984 Democratic National Convention said his knees were shaking "like an old washing machine."
- Actress Helen Hayes said she still suffered from stage fright after sixty years on Broadway.
- Tom Brokaw overcame a speech impediment before developing the comfortable, assured manner he demonstrates on his newscasts on NBC.

Dianne Gardner, professional speaker and author of *Gender Quotes: He Said, She Said,* put it very effectively: "Pushing through fear is less frightening than living with the underlying fear that comes from a feeling of helplessness. Evaluate your *satisfice* level. That's the point at which the satisfaction achieved justifies the sacrifices involved."

Earlier you began the process of self-knowledge about your stage fright. Now get very specific and use the following exercise to analyze the degree of your fear.

> *"Be a risk taker. Anything worth doing is worth doing poorly at first."*
>
> —Sheila Murray Bethel, speaker/author, *Making a Difference*

Speak Up and Stand Out

Exercise

Analyzing Your Fears: What Happens?

Mark the following possible reactions that apply to you when you speak before a group. Use the numbers 1 (severe), 2 (moderate), or 3 (minor) to identify the extent of your fearful physical, verbal, and nonverbal responses:

- ____ Light-headedness
- ____ Breathing distress
- ____ Queasy stomach
- ____ Dry mouth
- ____ Shaking (hands, knees, legs)
- ____ Trembling voice
- ____ Stuttering
- ____ Blushing
- ____ Pounding heart
- ____ Sweating (palms, underarms, face)
- ____ Verbal distractions
- ____ Repeating a word or phrases (including "Uh . . . " or "Mmmm . . .")
- ____ Unnatural posture (slumped or stiff)
- ____ Licking lips
- ____ Tapping foot

Facing the Fear

_____ Twisting or touching hair

_____ Scratching

_____ Pacing

_____ Losing eye contact

_____ Clicking fingernails

_____ Tapping fingers or pen or other item

_____ Unnatural hand gestures

_____ Putting hands in pockets to shake change or keys

Now that you've rated your reactions to fear, complete the following exercise to pinpoint when fear usually takes hold.

> *"Often people say their nervousness subsides 'once I get going.' If the first few seconds are typically your hardest, plan ahead and make them your easiest. Know exactly what you're going to say so you start off with a bang. Most people decide within the first few seconds how long they're going to listen to you. If you grab their attention and sense positive feedback immediately, it will give you a much-needed boost."*
>
> —Lynda Paulson, executive speech coach, Success Strategies, Inc.

Exercise

Analyze Your Fears: When Does It Happen?

Fears often follow a pattern of onset. Read through the descriptions below and use the following scale to mark the ones that apply: 1 = severe, 2 = moderate, and 3 = minor.

_____ In a meeting, when I think about the possibility of being asked to speak

_____ In the middle of planning, writing, and organizing a presentation

_____ Immediately prior to my presentation

_____ As I begin to speak

_____ After I start and think about what I'm doing

_____ After the whole thing is over and I think about how I did, the audience response, and so on

*According to a Stanford University study cited by Mary-Ellen Drummond (*Fearless and Flawless Public Speaking: With Power, Polish and Pizazz*), a person's success in life can be predicted by the way he or she responds to the question: "Are you willing to get up and give a speech right now?"*

Facing the Fear

Don't be discouraged by the numbers you've written. It's a place to start, helping you see your fear. There's an old saying that "a problem well defined is half solved." Once you find out what's going on and when, you can begin to see what you need to do.

You can minimize your suffering during stage fright, or even turn it into an advantage. Veteran actor Carroll O'Connor ("Archie Bunker") said this about stage fright: "A professional actor has a kind of tension. The amateur is thrown by it, but the professional needs it."

Control Your Breathing

Breath control is usually one of the first things to get out of whack when we experience strong emotions. So in order to deal with stage fright, you must have a plan for first equalizing your breathing, and the rest of your body will start to relax. Before your presentation, you can do a breathe-and-relax exercise that helps with many of the physical responses to fear. Of course, it's very effective when you're alone, but you can even use this technique when you're sitting on the stage or at the VIP table!

Here's how it goes:

1. Place your hands on the table or on your lap with palms down.

2. Wiggle, then relax, your hands and fingers.

3. Stretch out your legs; then place both feet flat on the floor.

4. Look slowly around the room; avoid focusing on any one person or object.

5. Close your eyes and let your body go completely limp.

6. Slowly inhale, taking a deep breath, and hold it for several seconds.

7. When you feel the urge to exhale, do so s-l-o-w-l-y.

8. Repeat the relaxed and slow inhale/exhale several times. Feel no hurry.

And there's more! Just imagine how the following would help:

- Wear comfy clothes.
- Empty your pockets and sew them up if you have to!
- Pick up objects like pens or pointers to use them, and then lay them down.
- Pause instead of uttering "mm . . ." or "uh . . ."
- Apply a light coat of Vaseline to your lips to keep them moist.
- Wear your hair out of your face.
- Have a coach (not a member of the family!) alert you in your practice sessions when you do distracting things.

"The way you overcome shyness is to become so wrapped up in something, you forget to be afraid," said Lady Bird Johnson. Smart lady!

Affirm Your Worth

Self-affirmations and visualizations help at every stage of fear. Create some self-affirming ideas that you can keep ready to repeat out loud or quietly to yourself as needed. Compose short sentences, using active verbs in the present tense and stated in positive terms. Like this:

- If I'm asked, great! I'll have a chance to share my ideas.
- I like being first because I can set the pace.

Facing the Fear

- Speaking is part of my job; it's what I do.
- I have good ideas that people need to hear.
- I research and ask others for ideas to make my presentation relevant.
- I practice and feel comfortable with the words I use.
- I feel at ease standing up and moving my hands and body.
- I smile and begin with confidence.
- I am overprepared, so I'm ready for a long or short version.
- I am a survivor and have a sense of humor for whatever happens!
- I have a backup plan in case my equipment fails.
- I am ready for questions, so I can help people.
- I am ready with questions, in case they don't ask any.
- I can do this.
- I am learning a new skill and doing better each time.

When you're feeling shaky and uncertain about your ability to rise to the challenge of public speaking, remember the strong words of Rudyard Kipling: "Of all the liars in the world, the worst are our own fears."

Visualize Your Worst Nightmare

Much of prepresentation jitters stems from "what ifs": What if I trip walking up to the lectern? What if I drop my notecards and they scatter out of order onto the floor? What if someone asks me a question I can't answer? The best strategy here is to fight fire with fire—let your imagination concoct a nightmare situation; then think about or jot down how you'd actually handle the situation. Following are a couple of examples to get you started.

Speak Up and Stand Out

Losing your train of thought:

- Take a sip of water; pause.
- Use humor—be honest and admit it.
- If that's enough to jog your memory, go on.
- If you really need help, ask your audience—they will love to encourage you.

Program runs long and you still have to speak:

- This is when preparation pays off! Know ahead of time what you'd cut.
- Don't try to give your planned presentation *faster*.
- Decide whether you can use your planned visual aids, or edit them as you go.
- Keep with your planned opener and closer.
- Alter the main points. Include only one point, or use all points but with only one example each.
- Don't blame, whine, or apologize.
- It's possible to make reference to "limited time," and then stick to it. Your audience knows what's going on. They appreciate your plight and your adaptability.
- Roll with the circumstances. You never know—it could improve your presentation.

> *"The difference between towering and cowering is how you hold yourself inside."*
>
> —Malcolm Forbes, Sr.,
> billionaire publisher

Facing the Fear

14

Create a Prepresentation Ritual

No serious athlete would dream of starting to jog, ride a bike, swim laps, or participate in any strenuous sport or physical activity without first warming up. Starting "cold" means a greater possibility of injury and/or a less than personal best result. Starting "warm" means the body and mind are responsive and ready to perform. Most professional athletes have developed a regular warm-up routine, which gets them focused and prepares the body and mind to work together.

Public speaking benefits from the same approach. Many professional speakers create a definite routine of activities that help equalize their breathing, relax their body, and get their mouth and voice warmed up. As you practice and, of course, actually speak before groups, you will create something that works for you. You'll learn that when you forget or get too confident, you generally don't perform at your peak. You'll also learn that when you *do* your routine, things work!

> **The "five P's" for professional presentations:**
> - Project positive thoughts.
> - Psyche yourself up.
> - Prepare thoroughly.
> - Practice properly.
> - Polish diligently.

Speak Up and Stand Out

two

Assessing Your Readiness for Success

Q. Can I be a successful presenter?

A. You can if you want to be.

The key is to assess your abilities and goals. That is, see your assets, determine what you have to work on, and make a commitment to improve. "Commitment" is an important element here; it's one of the "five C's for speaking success":

- Content (what you have to say, plus knowledge, skills, experiences)

- Communication (how you say it so people get it, plus vocal pitch, pace, tone, inflections, variety)

- Charisma (why people want to listen to you, plus energy, personality, style)

- Commitment (how much you want to do it, plus stamina, goal setting, willingness to practice)

- Character (why people should listen to you, plus "walking your talk," being your best)

Do you have a clear idea of where you are in this developmental process? Complete the following exercise to find out.

Speak Up and Stand Out

Exercise
Assessing Your Success Quotient

Read through the following lists and place a check next to the attributes that describe you right *now*:

Content

- [ ] Have ideas and interesting ways of looking at the world
- [ ] Know facts and figures other people would like to have
- [ ] Have skills others would like to acquire
- [ ] Can bring information together that is normally unrelated
- [ ] Have had one experience that is quite unusual
- [ ] Have accumulated a series of experiences that together make me different
- [ ] Have a personal victory story of winning against the odds
- [ ] Can organize ideas in a logical way
- [ ] Can explain things in simple terms
- [ ] Can see the funny side of things and share them

Communication

- [ ] Have had experiences that are universal, but people listen when I tell mine
- [ ] Know how to share a story to keep people listening

Assessing Your Readiness for Success

- ☐ Feel a surge of energy when talking about something I love
- ☐ Have creative ways of getting my point across
- ☐ Feel comfortable in my body
- ☐ Know people remember what I say
- ☐ Play my voice like an instrument, experimenting to see what is effective
- ☐ Change voice pitch and qualities to create other characters in stories I tell
- ☐ Feel comfortable using a microphone
- ☐ Feel comfortable away from the lectern

Charisma

- ☐ Can laugh and learn from daily experiences
- ☐ Am able to draw principles from a story to make a point
- ☐ Can laugh at myself
- ☐ Have an infectious laugh
- ☐ Make other people feel at ease
- ☐ Can create energy even when other people don't have it
- ☐ Have people tell me later that they took my advice
- ☐ Have stories people have heard before but love to hear again
- ☐ Have a bounce to my step
- ☐ Have an intensity or "sparkle" when I speak

Speak Up and Stand Out

Commitment

- [ ] Like the process of practice to improve a skill I want to improve
- [ ] Can manage my time and handle deadlines
- [ ] Am results oriented
- [ ] Can keep track and follow through on many details
- [ ] Am hungry to add to my knowledge in a specialty area
- [ ] Like to visualize and see the big picture or end goal
- [ ] Am interested in my personal and professional growth
- [ ] Look forward to attending classes and workshops
- [ ] Seek to know what's going on in the world
- [ ] Happily watch other presenters for ideas

Character

- [ ] Desire to be a good person (i.e., ethical, fair, conscientious)
- [ ] Find it easy to have a positive attitude when I'm with others, even difficult people
- [ ] Am flexible and keep my cool as I solve problems
- [ ] Know how to give credit to others and give attribution for ideas
- [ ] Am sensitive to situations and people's feelings and needs
- [ ] Can forget myself and focus on others
- [ ] Have a winning attitude about life

Assessing Your Readiness for Success

- [ ] Can graciously take feedback about my presentations whether or not I agree
- [ ] Am willing to audiotape myself, listen, be honest, and grow
- [ ] Am ready to videotape myself, watch, see myself as others see me, and learn

Once you've finished, total up your check marks in each of the "five C's" areas and fill in the spaces in the left column below. Multiply each total by two (as indicated) to derive a subscore for each area. Once that's done, sum your subscores for a grand total. That's your success I.Q.

_____ x 2 = Content

_____ x 2 = Communication

_____ x 2 = Charisma

_____ x 2 = Commitment

_____ x 2 = Character

TOTAL: _____

The total number of points you arrive at should tell you a lot. One hundred points would indicate total readiness. Since most of us wouldn't achieve a "perfect" score, the value of the results is to see how ready you are to work, change, practice, sweat, get feedback, not give up, and keep on keeping on!

"You can't sell 'em, if you can't tell 'em."
—Old sales motto

Speak Up and Stand Out

How ready and willing are you to do what it takes to *speak up and stand out?*

If your score is	Here's how you feel about public speaking
90 to 100	Volcanic!
80 to 89	Hot
70 to 79	Warm
60 to 69	Tepid
50 or less	Cool

Like just about every other skill in the world, whether it's tennis, tiddlywinks, triathlons, or teddy bear collecting, becoming a good speaker is largely a function of wanting to and being willing to pay the price. You can do an ability assessment, but the more critical components are motivation, practice, performance, feedback, and consistently better presentations. Each and every one of us can improve our public-speaking skills, guaranteed, no question! Just like any skill, you start where you are and target the next level.

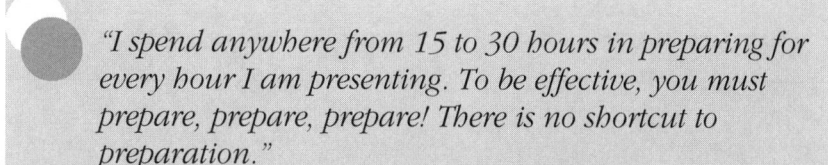

> "I spend anywhere from 15 to 30 hours in preparing for every hour I am presenting. To be effective, you must prepare, prepare, prepare! There is no shortcut to preparation."
>
> —Kay Johnson, speaker/trainer

Assessing Your Readiness for Success

Poor speakers	→	can become **Good** speakers
Good speakers	→	can become **Better** speakers
Better speakers	→	can become **Even better** speakers
Excellent speakers	→	can become **More polished and professional** speakers

Your goals and subsequent attitude will determine your progress. "Both tears and sweat are salty," said the Reverend Jesse Jackson, "but they render a different result. Tears will get you sympathy; sweat will get you change."

"Always have an ongoing education and self-development program."

—Mary-Ellen Drummond, speaker/author,
Fearless and Flawless Public Speaking with Power, Polish and Pizazz

Speak Up and Stand Out

three

Recognizing the Importance of Image

Q. *How can I look my best?*

A. *You use your natural gifts and work from there.*

No matter what you *intend* to convey to your listeners, their perception is their reality. When you stand up in front of people, what they see is what they get—are they getting what you want them to? Image consultant and speaker Gloria Boileau believes that your visual impact can make or break your career. One of her presentations has the apt title "I Didn't Mean What You Saw!"

John T. Molloy has given the world a series of books on the topic of dressing for success. People sometimes forget that *Dress for Success* and its sequels were not a prescription by Mr. Malloy on how you should dress if you want to be a success. On the contrary, these books drew on research into the kinds of judgments people make about each other based entirely on details of dress. Research participants were shown pictures and asked questions such as, What kind of job does this man/woman have? Salary? Education level? In other cases, people would enter an office and walk through, and then unsuspecting onlookers would be asked later to make certain judgments about the visitor based on appearance, clothing style and fabric, shoes, accessories, and so forth.

This is "reality," based on *perception*. When we first see a person, we have only the physical appearance to judge, and

Speak Up and Stand Out

judge we do! That's why our perception becomes our reality, unless something happens later to change our perception.

The First Seven Seconds

It doesn't take us long to register a visual image of someone, and that begins the process of interpreting what we see. This part takes only seven seconds. Seven seconds for visual stimuli to impress the brain and create a thought, which quickly yields a perceptual judgment. And that begins our "created" reality about that person.

People who are meeting "read" each other visually. This is how it works: You see. You process. You think. You get an impression. You have a feeling. You behave a certain way toward that person. The behavior triggers more thoughts and more feelings, and so it goes. This takes place in every visual human experience and is certainly happening when you watch a speaker stand before your group. Since visual stimuli are so powerful, "dressing for success" in public speaking is obviously part of the job of successful speakers!

Of those seven seconds, during the first four minutes the audience has formed an opinion about how your presentation is going. Your senses gather information along the following proportions:

- 87 percent by sight
- 7 percent by hearing
- 3.5 percent by smell
- 1.5 percent by touch
- 1 percent by taste

So what your audience sees is vitally important.

Recognizing the Importance of Image

The key here is dressing yourself to express the best, the most polished you. How you choose to dress speaks volumes about you, but it also says something about how you consider your audience. Your attire and appearance can communicate anything from "I was in a hurry and threw on any old thing" to "I took care to dress this way because it's a special occasion and you are important to me."

Remember, you are the message. (And part of *you* is what you have on, or don't have on!) When you're the speaker, here are some guidelines to steer your wardrobe and appearance choices:

- Dress appropriately for the occasion.
- Be among the best dressed in the room.
- Wear clean, pressed clothes that fit.
- Choose a good style to fit and enhance your body type.
- Go for a conservative, rather than trendy, style.
- Select the highest quality you can afford.
- Wear comfortable clothes that allow natural movement.
- Choose solid colors or barely discernible patterns.
- Darker colors are power colors.
- Navy blue is the most universally liked color.
- Select shoes that are comfortable, in good repair, and not overly noticeable.
- Your hair should be neat, not in your eyes or face.

More specific guidelines geared toward men and women are provided in the accompanying boxes.

Men

Men should be mindful of the following details:

- Dark, over-the-calf socks
- Dark shoes
- Conservative tie
- Limited amount of jewelry
- Good-quality belt

Women

In finishing their "look," women should note the following:

- Plain hosiery (no patterns)
- Pump-style shoes (no open toes or slingbacks), darker than the hemline
- Hemline at the knee or slightly below
- Conservative, classy (and not clanky) jewelry
- Medium-sized earrings (noticeable, not distracting)
- Rings limited to one per hand
- Nails manicured, not long, no bright polish
- Cosmetics in good taste, to enhance (not overdone)
- Hair in a style that keeps it out of the eyes, away from the face, and doesn't need to be moved, adjusted, pushed behind the ears, or fluffed (such distracting motions are the quickest way to conjure up images of Hollywood or high school)
- A jacket or blazer to add power

Recognizing the Importance of Image

A good guideline is to wear what looks good on you and makes you feel comfortable and yet is "classy." That's it: comfortable class. This winning combination will free you to forget about yourself, so you readily focus on your audience and what you have to say. The right clothes, the right look, to send the right message at the right time, is the right thing to do. There really is no other option if you're serious about speaking up and standing out for the right reason!

> *"Charisma is the intangible that makes people want to follow you, to be around you, to be influenced by you."*
>
> —Roger Dawson, speaker/author,
> *Secrets of Power Persuasion*

four

Polishing the Sounds of Successful Speaking

Q. *What about my voice?*

A. *Your voice is saying more than words.*

Your voice is so personal, so qualitatively unique, that its sound can be used as a security code. It's an audible fingerprint, your vocal signature. Voicing happens in three actions:

- Inhalation (bringing air into the lungs)
- Exhalation (releasing air from the lungs)
- Sound production

The latter occurs when the air brought in during inhalation passes through your larynx, or voice box. Though the action itself is commonplace, individual uniqueness results from your very specific and personal combination of volume, pitch, tone, rate, timbre, and inflection. Add to that the words you use—the way you pronounce them as well as the particular words and phrases you select, and how you put them together—and the resulting package is one of a kind.

Public speaking, by definition, means you are up in front of people generating sounds, and the way you do that can create a personal connection or disconnection. Some sounds turn people off to ideas; others turn them on, or at least don't get in the way.

Your voice is the physical medium of your message. To the listener, your voice then becomes intertwined with your message. Your voice serves as the audible package that carries your ideas.

According to research done by communications expert Dr. Albert Mehrabian at UCLA, interpersonal communication in its entirety is comprised of the following:

- Verbal (word selection, syntax, etc.): 7 percent
- Vocal (volume, pitch, tone, rate, etc.): 38 percent
- Visual (body language and facial expression): 55 percent

In other words, more than one-third of your interpersonal communication success depends on *your voice*.

Listen to Yourself

The first step to improving any ability is assessment—if you find out where you are now, you're better able to determine where you're going. In the case of your voice, the obvious starting point is to *listen*. Tape yourself! Choose one or preferably all three of the following options:

- Tape yourself in conversation with someone on the phone. Call up a friend, have your tape recorder close by, and turn it on so you only get *your* side of the conversation.

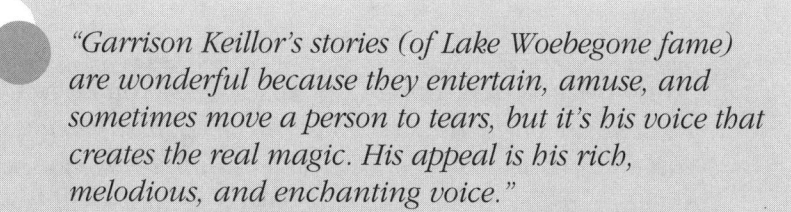

> *"Garrison Keillor's stories (of Lake Woebegone fame) are wonderful because they entertain, amuse, and sometimes move a person to tears, but it's his voice that creates the real magic. His appeal is his rich, melodious, and enchanting voice."*
>
> —Joanne Sherman, contributing writer to *The Toastmaster,* in an article, "Beauty is in the Ear of the Listener"

Polishing the Sounds of Successful Speaking

- Tape a letter to a friend. Keep it chatty. Talk about things that are important to you, but not too personal. Give opinions. Share something you just read or heard on the news. Decide later if you actually want to send it.
- Tape your next presentation.

Now sit down, listen to your tapes, and assess your voice overall, keeping in mind the circumstances. You can always enlist another person's help in this project too. Choose someone you trust and feel comfortable with. (Probably a good choice would be someone not related to you.)

The following exercise provides checklists of descriptions that will help you pinpoint a variety of your vocal attributes.

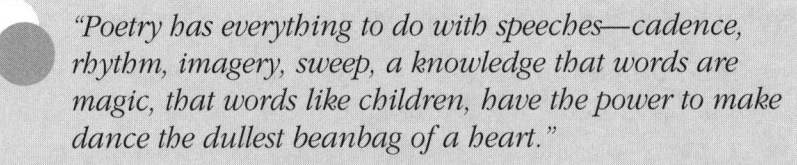

> *"Poetry has everything to do with speeches—cadence, rhythm, imagery, sweep, a knowledge that words are magic, that words like children, have the power to make dance the dullest beanbag of a heart."*
>
> —Peggy Noonan, author/speechwriter to President Ronald Reagan

> *"You always sound louder to yourself than you do to the audience. Double your volume and see how inflection and energy increase. A louder voice commands more attention and respect. Burn off nervous energy with vocal power."*
>
> —Phillip Stella, Effective Training and Communication, Inc.

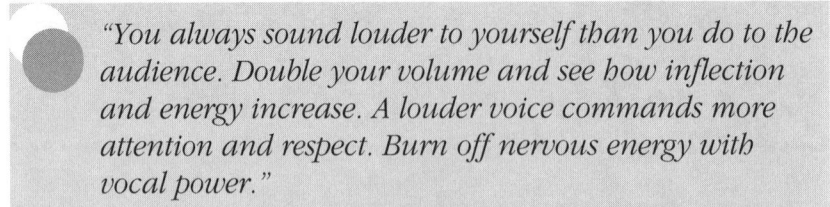

Speak Up and Stand Out

Exercise
Assessing Your Voice Qualities

1. Listening to tapes you have made of yourself, place a check mark next to each item you feel you could improve with regard to your vocal quality.

   Rate or pace:
   - ☐ Could be faster
   - ☐ Could be slower
   - ☐ About right

   Variety in rate or pace:
   - ☐ Significant
   - ☐ Some
   - ☐ Very little

   Volume:
   - ☐ Could be louder
   - ☐ Could be softer
   - ☐ About right

   Variety in volume:
   - ☐ Significant
   - ☐ Some change
   - ☐ Little change

Polishing the Sounds of Successful Speaking

Pitch:

- ☐ Too high
- ☐ Too low
- ☐ About right

Variety in pitch:

- ☐ Significant
- ☐ Some change
- ☐ Little change

2. Write down any repetitious words and phrases you tend to use (include "uhs," ums," etc.):

   _____
   _____
   _____
   _____
   _____
   _____
   _____
   _____
   _____

3. Describe your voice:

   - ☐ Small, thin, whispery
   - ☐ Soft, timid
   - ☐ Big, booming

- [ ] Loud, gruff
- [x] Nasal
- [x] Hesitating, halting
- [ ] Whiny
- [ ] Screechy, shrill
- [ ] Strident, pushy
- [x] Smooth, mellow
- [x] Average, just a voice
- [ ] Friendly, animated
- [ ] Detached, matter-of-fact
- [ ] Breathy
- [ ] Squeaky
- [x] Relaxed, pleasant
- [ ] Tight, forced
- [ ] Good use of "pause"
- [ ] Run-on words
- [ ] Word endings chopped off (playin', teachin', doin')
- [ ] Understandable, good diction

4. Rate yourself overall:
   - [ ] If I were not me, I would find it hard to listen to me.
   - [ ] If I were not me, I would find it easy to listen to me.

Polishing the Sounds of Successful Speaking

5. Review your responses to the previous questions, and then summarize your strengths as well as areas for improvement.

Good things about my voice:

_____
_____
_____
_____
_____
_____
_____
_____

Things to work on:

_____
_____
_____
_____
_____
_____
_____
_____

Once you've pinpointed your rough spots or weak areas, it's time to get to work.

Improving Your Vocal Delivery

The goal here is to alter various aspects of your vocal delivery in specific, identifiable ways, to increase the likelihood of your message being received and understood as intended. Some people adopt an aggressive approach, taking speech classes or working with a speech consultant/coach. It's also possible to work on your voice all by yourself. Following are some exercises for maximizing your message with your voice.

1. Pronounce these words two times each, and then go over the list again:

   education (ed-you-CAY-shun)

   government (listen for the "n")

   manufacture (man-you-FAC-chur)

   hundred (HUN-dread)

   fifth (listen for the middle "f")

   library (LIE-brer-ee)

2. Say these words and make the endings "ring!" Do so twice, first normally and then a second time "with feeling":

playing	singing
ringing	flinging
winging	inning
maximizing	

> *"The actor has only three assets—voice, body, and personality."*
>
> —Charlton Heston, actor

Polishing the Sounds of Successful Speaking

3. Practice enunciating the final consonant sounds in these words. Repeat the list three times, increasing your speed each time:

help	dead
sock	dot
barb	start
gag	kick
unique	fox

4. Practice the final "s" sound in these words. Say them twice, first slowly, and then quickly. The second time touch lightly but firmly on the end:

slice	nice
mice	entice
advice	chance
advance	enhance
slow dance	fast dance
kiss	miss
abyss	success

5. Practice articulating the terminal "z" sound in these words. Say them twice and enjoy the "buzz" on your teeth:

buzz	fuzz
fizz	gee whiz
monkeys	materials
maladies	tirades

Speak Up and Stand Out

maintains   streams

reams   bags

nags

6. Practice the "ch" sound in these words. Give the drill some energy, going twice through the list:

choo choo   cha cha

chuck   chasten

church   chimney

cheek   charming

munch   bunch

lunch

7. Go twice through this next list, having fun saying the words and listening carefully to the different ways the vowels sound:

bah, boil, beau, boo, beautiful

rack, wreck, rock, rucksack, rook

mate, mote, mute, moot

mane, mean, moan, moon, immune

pill, pile, appealing, appalling, apparent

8. Say the following sentences with energy, filling in the blanks as appropriate. Take care to avoid *uptalk*, the tendency to sound like you're asking a question rather than stating a fact:

Hi, my name is _____.

I work for _____.

Polishing the Sounds of Successful Speaking

I've been there for _____ (months/years).

My job title is _____.

I'm here today because I wanted to
_____.

9. Breathe from the diaphragm, keeping your shoulders down and chin up, and then do the following (this is a great prepresentation breath control warm-up):

   - Yawn—a big, bold, extravagant, dramatic yawn!
   - Open your mouth wide and say "Ahh . . ." four times.
   - Follow a tip from voice instructor Janet Smith at Chapman University. Take a full breath over four counts; then expel it slowly and consistently, making a steady hissing sound. Time how many seconds you can keep the hissing constant without straining. Next, take the breath to a count of three and repeat the process, then to a count of two, and finally to a count of one. "You learn to relax, to open those muscles," Smith says. A first-timer with this exercise will likely be able to hiss no longer than eighteen to twenty seconds.

10. Select some passages—poetry, narrative, scenes from a play—and read aloud, with feeling. Enhance the meaning of each selection by pausing and using variety in your tone, inflection, rate, and volume.

> *"A presentation is a one-on-one conversation with a lot of people simultaneously."*
>
> —Don Gabor, speaker/author, *How to Start a Conversation and Make Friends*

Speak Up and Stand Out

Take Care of Your Voice

Finally, it's very important to take care of your voice. Follow these tips and you'll never have to sing the vocal blues:

- *Talk first, eat later.* Your body can't digest food and support your speaking at the same time.

- *On presentation day, choose foods wisely.* Stay with healthy, easily digested foods such as fruits, vegetables, fish, and pasta. Stay away from heavy, high-fat foods and meats. Avoid milk products (they increase mucous production). Carbonated drinks and caffeine? Save them until after you speak.

- *No smoking allowed.* Besides the familiar health concerns, speakers should avoid smoking for other reasons too. It dries out your mouth, nose, and throat and can lead to frequent throat clearing, which in turn irritates the vocal cords. Secondhand smoke can irritate your voice as well. If you can't avoid it before the speech, gargle with saltwater to eliminate dryness and excess mucous.

- *Save your voice—project from the diaphragm.* If you try to sound louder by taking a big breath from your shoulders and chest, but then push on the throat, you'll only irritate it and eventually lose your voice. For louder sound as well as breath support, go lower, using the muscles in your abdomen and your diaphragm.

- *Warm up your speaking voice by singing softly.* The gentle hum and vibration of your vocal cords will warm them up without straining them. Just sing a round of "Happy Birthday" or "You Are My Sunshine."

Polishing the Sounds of Successful Speaking

- *Keep a drink of water handy to lubricate your throat.* Though room temperature is best, just avoid anything very hot or icy cold.

- *If you think you're losing your voice, rest it completely.* That is, don't talk! Don't even whisper; just use pen and paper. Your voice will recover faster if you rest the muscles at the first sign of a problem.

Down With Uptalk!

Uptalk is the tendency to use rising intonations at the end of a sentence or phrase even when the speaker is not asking a question. According to James Gorman, professor of journalism, New York University, *uptalk* has a tendency to leave the listener with the impression that the speaker is tentative, unauthoritative, and unsure. Cynthia McLemore, linguist, University of Pennsylvania and frequent contributor to National Public Radio, says it's a spreading phenomenon, most common among teenagers.

Writing in the *New York Times* for the William Safire "On Language" column, Gorman says it's not just teens. He says he heard himself say, "Hi, This is Jim Gorman? I'm doing an article on Kling-on? The language? From 'Star Trek'?" He realized that he was unwittingly, unwillingly speaking *uptalk.* Then he adds, "I was, like, appalled?" Think about how it would have sounded if veteran news anchor Walter Cronkite had closed his newscasts with, "And that's the way it is?"

Speak Up and Stand Out

five

Tapping the Power of Body Language

Q. *What do I do about my hands and arms, and where I stand, and how much I move?*

A. *Body talk speaks the loudest of all.*

As described in Chapter 4, you share more than half your message through what you do with your hands, body, eyes, and face! When the words and body language don't match, people tend to believe the body language.

Easy Does It and Natural Is Nice

One beginning speaker complained, "I never even noticed what I do with my hands when I talk until I stood in front of an audience. All of a sudden they seemed heavy and in the way. I felt awkward making the slightest gesture. It took several speaking experiences before I began to feel at home with my hands and body during a presentation."

Hand gestures have five important uses and benefits in public speaking:

- To emphasize main points
- To help the group follow your presentation and train of thought
- To help your listeners better "see" your examples
- To show the people just how relaxed (or not) you are
- To demonstrate how much energy and enthusiasm you have for your topic

Speak Up and Stand Out

Your natural body language, which includes your gestures, eye contact, facial expressions, posture, and presence, is nothing more than a manifestation of your internal feelings. The words you say and how you say them are important, yes, and can require your careful preparation. However, body language, in some ways more important, is often the last to be remembered and practiced, and the first to be noticed if it doesn't match, mirror, or enhance the total presentation.

To see just how "talkative" body language can be, observe the speaker very closely at the next presentation you attend. Is what he or she is doing so "loud" that you can't hear a word that person is saying? Do his or her gestures convey a message like the following?

- "My message is clear—simple as one, two, three—and I believe every word I'm saying."

- "What I have to say is so important, you'll want to keep listening."

- "Here is information so enlightening, you'll get excited too."

- "This is my personal experience, and here's what helped me."

- "Use this strategy and you'll definitely have a better meeting."

- "The number one reason you need this new idea (plan, product, etc.) is . . . "

Or do they broadcast something more like the following?

- "I don't know why they asked me to talk—there are other people who know more about this."

Tapping the Power of Body Language

- "I was assigned to give this stuff, but I think everyone here already knows most of it anyway."
- "My clothes don't really feel comfortable and my shoes are killing me."
- "I'm really scared. I'll hold onto this lectern for support. I'm afraid to come out from behind it."
- "I think you're all a bunch of dips because you don't know this already."
- "I'm completely uncomfortable up here and can't wait to sit down."

Do's and Don'ts

After one or more such observation exercises, picture yourself standing before your audience. Following are some body language guidelines.

Hands

- *Do* move them when you have a reason, as natural extensions to your message.
- *Do* keep them looking spontaneous.
- *Do* keep your gestures high enough to be seen (large groups will require larger gestures).
- *Do* vary your gestures so you don't overly use or depend on one favorite.
- *Do* keep them at your side sometimes if it feels natural.
- *Do* use an open hand, facing up, when referring to individuals in the room.
- *Do* use one hand at your side, one arm bent at the waist.

- *Do* use the *steeple* gesture at waist level (hands clasped, pointer fingers touching).
- *Do* use the *birdcage* gesture at waist level (fingers extended, ends touching).
- *Do not* scratch where it itches.
- *Do not* touch your face excessively.
- *Do not* stroke, fluff, or twist your hair.
- *Do not* fiddle with objects.
- *Do not* point to people with one finger.
- *Do not* keep hands in the *fig leaf* or *reversed fig leaf* position (crossed in front or in back).

Legs, feet

- *Do* plant your feet firmly on the ground.
- *Do* place your feet six to twelve inches apart, depending on how natural it feels and looks.
- *Do* keep your legs flexible and ready to move.
- *Do not* remove your shoes.
- *Do not* wrap one foot around or on top of the other.
- *Do not* place one foot on a chair.
- *Do not* bend one leg, resting on the other too often.
- *Do not* tap or jiggle a foot in nervousness.

Body

- *Do* increase your physical space.
- *Do* stand erect, shoulders back but natural.

- *Do* tuck your pelvis in and pull your waist up out of your hips.
- *Do* evenly distribute your weight.
- *Do* use smooth moves.
- *Do* move your body when you gesture with your hand and arm.
- *Do* feel free to walk around closer to your audience.
- *Do not* adjust your clothing.
- *Do not* repeatedly pull at your cuffs, tie, jewelry, scarf, etc.
- *Do not* invade people's "space."
- *Do not* touch anyone without asking.
- *Do not* pace in a predictable pattern.
- *Do not* weave or rock back and forth.

Head, face

- *Do* hold your head erect, with your chin parallel to the floor.
- *Do* use natural movements and expressions.
- *Do* not tilt your head to one side when giving information.
- *Do not* use mannerisms that are distracting: head jerks, excessive grimacing, licking lips, etc.

According to Rick Jordan's article "The Face of Feeling" in *Psychology Today*, there are eighty muscles in the face capable of making more than 7,000 different expressions. That ought to give any speaker enough variety for his or her presentation!

Speak Up and Stand Out

Eye contact

- *Do* look at individuals.
- *Do* hold their attention for one to three seconds.
- *Do* vary the sections of the audience you look at and the duration of the contact.
- *Do* accompany eye contact with an appropriate nod or other movements.
- *Do not* look only at the same individual(s) again and again.
- *Do not* hold eye contact for four or more seconds, unless it's part of your content.
- *Do not* look above the listeners' heads, especially in groups of twenty-five or less.
- *Do not* just mechanically scan the audience like an oscillating fan.
- *Do not* look up to the ceiling for noticeable periods of time.
- *Do not* look at an individual and then glance at your watch.
- *Do not* use quick, frenetic eye movements.

Several simple exercises can help you develop your natural body language:

- Practice a segment of your presentation in front of a mirror, even if you can only see part of yourself. You'll get an idea of what hand gestures look spontaneous and natural.
- Tell one of your stories while standing in the middle of your living room, facing your front window (your audience!). Mark off at least a six-square-foot area with furniture or masking tape. During your story, naturally move to every section of that space.

Tapping the Power of Body Language

- Give your three main points to a "friendly" wall and consciously use your hands, fingers, and body to sell those three ideas.

- Loosen up your gestures. A larger audience will need this, and don't worry—very few people tend to overdo it in the real presentation! Stand in an open space and practice making very large, exaggerated gestures for these comments:

"There is a new phenomenon sweeping the country."

"If this plan (product, idea, strategy) could save you money, would you be interested?"

"I've never seen weather like this in my life!"

"Imagine what it would have been like to be Sir Edmund Hilary, the first person in the world to stand on top of Mt. Everest, the world's tallest mountain peak."

As Jan Carlzon summed it up in *Moments of Truth,* "leadership communication . . . involves more than a little showmanship. If you want to be an effective leader, you cannot be shy or reticent. Knowing how to appear before large audiences and persuade them 'to buy' your message is a crucial attribute of leadership—almost as crucial as being able to calculate or plan."

> *"Consummate professionals are 'one with the audience.' They 'walk in the audiences' moccasins' and make each presentation fit the environment."*
>
> —Denis Waitley, motivational speaker,
> *Psychology of Winning, Seeds of Greatness*

six

Identifying Your Objectives

Q. *Where do I start?*

A. *First, decide what you want to accomplish.*

Presentations by their nature exemplify *communication with an objective.* No matter how informal, presentations still are structured to be more than a speaker before an audience chatting away randomly. There is a reason why a certain speaker stands before the group—and within a very short period of time, it ought to be obvious to the members of the group. However, the objective of the presentation can only be obvious to the listeners if it's perfectly clear to the speaker!

There are four main categories of speech objectives:

- Inform
- Persuade
- Motivate
- Entertain

In reality, it's almost impossible to separate these into neat little divisions and demonstrate that any one presentation has only *one* express purpose. You can have one main, overarching purpose for the occasion, but most of the time a combination of objectives exists.

Speak Up and Stand Out

For example, an effective presentation to *inform* also needs elements of *motivation* in order to *persuade* listeners to use the information, and *humor* and *an entertaining style* could help them better remember the material.

Try the following exercise for practice in identifying possible presentation objectives.

> *"Whether your forum is a corporate boardroom or a PTA meeting, your degree of speaking skill will determine to a great extent how seriously people take your ideas and whether they'll follow your lead."*
>
> —Aram Bakshian, editor,
> *American Speaker*

> *"Speak from the heart, not just the mind. Concentrate on benefits to others, and your message must be entertaining and carry interesting stories to make your substance digestible."*
>
> —Cavett Robert, president emeritus and co-founder of the U.S. National Speakers Association

Identifying Your Objectives

Exercise

Analyzing Possible Objectives

Let's consider some examples of reasons why speakers stand before groups, and then analyze the objective or possible combination of objectives. Some examples are indicated; you fill in the rest to get the idea how very few objectives are cut and dried.

Main objective(s) = X; additional objective(s) = x:

Do I want them: Then I'll need to:

	Inform	Motivate	Persuade	Entertain
1. To know all about an upcoming event and want to be there?	X	x	X	?
2. To know a situation needs helping hands and get them to volunteer to pitch in?	X	x	X	?
3. To buy something?	x	x	X	?
4. To laugh and feel happy and enjoy being together as a group?				X

Speak Up and Stand Out

	Inform	Motivate	Persuade	Entertain
5. To be able to demonstrate a certain skill or operate a piece of equipment?	X	x	x	
6. To donate money or equipment?	x	X	X	
7. To understand all the implications of a situation or decision?	X			
8. To budget enough money for a certain project?	x	x	X	
9. To feel sympathetic to a person's plight?	x	X		
10. To feel irritated or upset at a new policy and sign a petition?	x	X	X	

Identifying Your Objectives

	Inform	Motivate	Persuade	Entertain
11. To question the veracity of a certain fact or report?	X			?
12. To understand all the advantages and disadvantages of a strategy?	X			
13. To desire to improve their use of time?	x	X	X	
14. To care about a cause such as recycling or pollution and change their habits?	X	x	X	
15. To exercise regularly, eat properly, and get enough sleep?	x	X	X	?
16. To appreciate the sacrifice of one individual and feel inspired on a solemn occasion?	x	X		

Speak Up and Stand Out

	Inform	Motivate	Persuade	Entertain
17. To get the boss to authorize a weekend retreat for the workers in the department?				
18. To worry about saving for college (retirement, home etc.) and open an account and sock away $25 per month?				
19. To restore faith in the system, the agency, or the plan?				
20. To lighten up and not take the situation, life, things so seriously?				

Identifying Your Objectives

Bottom line, public speaking is results oriented. Determine at the outset precisely what you want your listeners to leave with, and your ultimate purpose will be clear:

- Facts, figures, trends, information that fleshes out their knowledge on a topic? (INFORM)
- Strong desire to take a course of action and a plan to implement it? (PERSUADE)
- Powerful feelings from emotional experiences and stories, which they remember long after your speech? (MOTIVATE)
- A memory of a great, fun, relaxing time together? (ENTERTAIN)

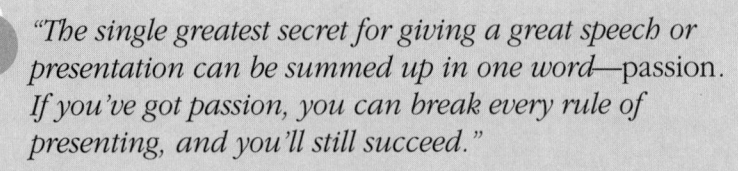

> *"The single greatest secret for giving a great speech or presentation can be summed up in one word—passion. If you've got passion, you can break every rule of presenting, and you'll still succeed."*
>
> —Bryan Mattimore, speaker/author,
> *99% Inspiration*

Speak Up and Stand Out

seven

Anticipating Your Audience

Q. *How can I best reach my audience?*

A. *Analyze them; take a look at those looking back at you.*

Best-selling author Harvey Mackay *(Swim With the Sharks Without Being Eaten Alive; Beware the Naked Man Who Offers You His Shirt; Sharkproof)* is dogmatic about preparation. Before he accepts any invitation to speak, he goes to great lengths to get to know his audience, using a questionnaire he originally developed to get to know clients. "I use the 'Mackay 66,' which is a sixty-six-question customer profile to find out everything I can about the group I'll be addressing. That includes demographics, interests, political affiliations, favorite speakers, past successful topics, anything I can use when I step up to the podium."

Know Before You Go

Following is the kind of information you'll want to obtain before you even begin planning or adapting your presentation:

- Requested topic
- Name of person, group, client, department, and so on
- Liaison's name
- Phone numbers (work, home)
- Date of presentation

Speak Up and Stand Out

- Location/address/building/room number (including mailing address, if different)
- Directions for easy arrival
- Occasion
- Food/refreshments planned
- Attendance (how many; voluntary vs. required)
- Other speakers
- What happens before presentation
- Time allowed for presentation
- Q & A wanted? Part of allotted time, or extra time? How much?
- Announced title of presentation
- Person introducing me (need to furnish an introduction?)
- Description of facilities, room, and setup for presentation
- Equipment availability (microphone/type; audiovisual aids/type)

Getting clear answers to the above questions gives you powerful knowledge. You really have a great picture of what the situation is going to be and how your part will fit in.

Next you need to compile very specific information about who will be there. Because each situation will be different, skip any of the following elements that don't apply:

- Size of audience (number or percentage of men and women)
- Age range
- Occupations/job titles/positions
- Years of experience

Anticipating Your Audience

- Nature of organization or industry
- Attendees with the most authority in the organization
- Education levels
- Cultural diversity
- Knowledge of subject (beginning/intermediate/advanced)
- Other presentations they've had on this subject
- Why topic was selected for this group
- Specific objectives and/or ideas group should learn from presentation
- Any critical issues that need to be covered
- Any topic or issue to avoid
- Trends affecting this group
- Issues or opportunities facing group now
- Group's relationship to each other (e.g., they work together every day; they rarely see each other but work closely via e-mail; they are area managers from various places, etc.)
- Name and position of one person in the organization the group communicates with most often
- Expectations of the group
- General attitude toward me (known/unknown/friendly/hostile/indifferent)
- Perceived credibility on subject (high/medium/low)
- Any recent event, situation, or local color to take into consideration
- Anything humorous happening lately that affected the group (refer to this in presentation)

- Kinds of examples, stories, personal anecdotes, or historical references group would appreciate most
- Anything else about group that would help me prepare and deliver my presentation

Using What You Know About Your Audience

Once you have an idea about the people who will be looking back at you, it's your job to present your information in a way that they want to listen to! The most important thing to remember is their favorite "radio station": WII-FM. That's shorthand for the question they are asking themselves: WHAT'S IN IT FOR ME? What's in this that I can use, need, or care about? Cavett Robert, president emeritus of the National Speakers Association, penned the following humorous picture of WII-FM:

The audience is sitting

Like owls up in a tree.

Big round eyes are asking us,

What's in this talk for me?

Considering and remembering the following main points makes a great difference:

- **How many?** The number of people in your audience does affect the style of the presentation. It also changes the listeners' expectations. That is, if a group is small, they will expect you to be more informal, perhaps offering more interaction. The larger the group, the more formal the situation tends to become and thus the less interactive. Good speakers learn to adapt their delivery style, voice

Anticipating Your Audience

projection and diction, word choice, and certainly body language to the size of the group and situation. Group size has the most obvious effect on your choice and use of visual aids (see Chapter 9).

- **Male, female, mixed groups?** Knowing the gender mix of your audience can influence the kind of examples, analogies, and metaphors you use. Although sports metaphors are common in business, it's a good habit to select stories that are really universal. Much research has been done in the field of gender communication, and scientists, psychologists, and linguists alike show evidence that the genders tend to differ in the way they listen and process information.

  Deborah Tannen, linguist and author of *You Just Don't Understand,* indicates that women are more likely than men to give more eye contact, nods, and smiles, and speakers quickly learn to look to the women in the audience for the obvious signs of attention. This doesn't mean, however, that the women really *are* listening or are even in agreement—this is a common misperception. Another misperception is that because men tend to give less eye contact, appear to be less focused, and exhibit more closed body language, they are not listening. *It doesn't necessarily mean that at all!* Studies show that women tend be able to handle both the process and the content of a situation; men tend to do one or the other.

  Very importantly, avoid sexist language. Rephrase statements to include men and women or use neutral descriptive terms. For example, say "workforce" instead of "manpower," "supervisor" instead of "foreman," "artificial" or even "manufactured" instead of "man-made."

- **Age range?** Age categories will indicate the eras and general experiences your audience members have lived through and the associated facts they share. The best advice here is to know their heroes, their role models. Don't assume, however, that all members of your audience share the same perspective on life, relationships, or even historical events.

- **Education and experience?** Just as knowing the gender and age range of your audience is vital to your speech preparation so is knowing the general education and experience level. These aspects influence the content of your presentation tremendously—you'll need to adapt your word choice, your selection of examples, how much detail your explanations include, and how much business or industry "jargon" and acronyms you can safely use. People can get very frustrated and will turn you off if you obviously talk above or below their knowledge level.

- **Cultural diversity? language?** Cultural diversity is more and more a consideration for the public speaker. People don't appreciate negative stereotyping, and an insensitive speaker can lose credibility immediately and quickly turn a friendly or neutral audience into a hostile one. Be particularly careful in your uses of humor (see Chapter 8). If English is not the first language of your audience members, or if you are speaking through an interpreter, it is imperative to slow down, emphasize your diction, and keep it simple. (Actually, that's good advice for *any* situation!)

The goal of audience analysis is to "know" the people looking back at you. It's an interesting phenomenon, because it's the essence of empathy and understanding. When the connection happens, you feel it, they feel it, and the time together seems

Anticipating Your Audience

incredibly well spent. If the presentation starts out with your audience impressed with you and your knowledge of them or your subject, that's commendable, but remember the real goal is what Bob Pike, trainer extraordinaire, says: "I believe people should leave impressed with themselves."

Troubleshooting "People" Situations

Public speaking sometimes involves dealing with "gremlins" in the gathering or other uncomfortable people-related circumstances. Following are some common examples as well as tips for handling them.

Hecklers and nasties:

- Keep your temper in check. Don't give in to provocation.
- If you are polite, the audience will be on your side (often audiences let the people know the behavior is unappreciated).
- Ignore the person first, briefly. If that doesn't work, then give him or her the attention sought by asking in a casual, polite voice, "Did you have a question?"
- Though rarely needed, you might want to have a "polite, professional bouncer."

"Experts," "know-it-alls," and "live ones"

- Make it a point early on to call on such people often. That way, you control when they comment.
- Ask other audience members their opinions; this shows you won't allow one person to dominate.

- If this person has contributed several times, watch responses from other audience members. The minute you see even one person roll his or her eyes or give some other sign, you'll know to stop including this "expert" or "know-it-all."
- If this person continues to raise his or her hand, just ignore it.
- If this person speaks out without being recognized, keep your gaze directed at another section of the audience and ignore the person.
- A big help may be to limit the number of questions you ask the group.

Chatty people:

- Draw talkers back into your presentation by asking for comments or opinions.
- Look directly at the talkers while you're speaking. Maintain eye contact just slightly longer than normal. Important: Keep it friendly.
- When you have a wireless mike, the most effective strategy can be to casually walk over toward the chatty folks and stand close by while talking to the rest of the group and casting your eyes around (*including* friendly eye contact with the chatterers). Doing this nonchalantly, but with purpose, helps!

Late arrivals:

- Ignore them.
- Welcome them to empty seats.

- Don't assume everyone who comes in late is impolite; it could be they were caught up in traffic, lost, or delayed for some other legitimate reason.

- Don't start over again to cover what late arrivals missed. Check with them at the break to fill in gaps.

Conflicting audience attitudes, values, and beliefs:

- Downplay differences by focusing on points of agreement; then move on.

- If the conflict is unfounded, or the listener misunderstood, ask for clarification and then show how you really are in agreement.

- Casually call on someone in the audience who's an expert or has firsthand experience in the area of the dispute. As a third party, that person may serve as a mediator or peacemaker.

- Remain upbeat and positive.

- Show—through your voice and body language—how enthusiastic you are about your ideas or plans.

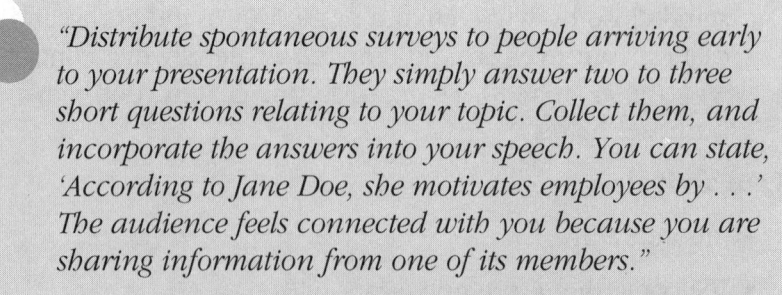

> *"Distribute spontaneous surveys to people arriving early to your presentation. They simply answer two to three short questions relating to your topic. Collect them, and incorporate the answers into your speech. You can state, 'According to Jane Doe, she motivates employees by . . .' The audience feels connected with you because you are sharing information from one of its members."*
>
> —Silvana Clark, speaker/author,
> *Taming the Marketing Jungle*

Question-and-Answer Survival Kit

One of the best mental tools you can give yourself in the area of anticipating your audience is a "question-and-answer survival kit":

1. **A plan.** As you prepare your presentation, anticipate the questions you might receive. Write out responses and practice answering them.

2. **A vision.** See yourself fielding questions with finesse. You are knowledgeable on this topic.

3. **A positive attitude.** Think of questions as opportunities to share more important information with your audience members.

Following are some additional points to consider and to practice in maximizing this exchange with your audience:

- Treat the Q & A period as part of your presentation. Do not lower your energy level.

- Gear the Q & A session to the objectives you want to accomplish.

- Look directly at the person asking the question. Give him or her a pleasant, thoughtful look.

- Listen carefully, for both content and feeling, by observing facial expressions and body language.

- Thank the person for the question. Affirmations such as the following signal a positive acknowledgment:

    "That's an interesting question . . ."

    "You make a good point, Susan . . ."

    "I'm glad you are bringing this to our attention . . ."

    "You've obviously given this a lot of thought . . ."

Anticipating Your Audience

- Look at the entire audience when answering.

- Always paraphrase the question before you answer. Doing so helps those who didn't hear it, gives the person asking the question an opportunity to clarify if you misunderstood, and extends you more time to think of an answer.

- Treat two questions from the same person as two separate questions.

- Rotate the way you select questions from the audience. Let individuals seated in all areas of the room have a chance to speak.

- Avoid negative body language. No hands on hips or folded over your chest while you're listening. Keep the same ready-to-speak stance throughout.

- Avoid answering with such phrases as "Well, obviously . . ." or "As I said in my talk, . . ."

- Extend your arm with hand facing up to gesture to the questioner. No pointy fingers!

- Be diplomatic when handling objections:
    - Don't try to prove you're right.
    - Acknowledge the person's viewpoint.
    - Use this opportunity to clarify your ideas.
    - Agree, if the person is right.
    - Don't get caught up in a dispute that sacrifices your rapport with the audience, compromises your credibility, and upsets your composure.

Speak Up and Stand Out

For large groups, ask members to write down their questions and submit them beforehand (if the topic or your format permits them to anticipate questions in advance of the presentation). For very large groups, you may need an extra mike for Q & A.

- For medium to large groups, have the person asking the question to stand.

- Remain in control of the session. Do not let it drag on or fizzle out. Keep within the time limits set by the program chair. When you're nearly out of time, say, "There's time for one more question . . ."

- Save one last "clincher" statement or a dynamic ending to bring effective closure to the session. These last words should be brief but powerful: Your Super Closer!

- Be available afterwards. People love accessibility to a speaker they've enjoyed or been stimulated by, plus here's additional opportunities to spread your message. Keep up your energy—the session isn't over until the last member of the audience is out the door!

> *"I like to get people involved from the beginning. I meet as many people as possible at the beginning of the day. I call for volunteers to model behaviors. I use break-out sessions and prizes."*
>
> —Gloria Boileau, speaker/trainer

Anticipating Your Audience

eight

Writing Your Speech

Q. *Writing the speech sounds like work. Can you make it easy?*

A. *It's as easy as one, two, three.*

Three is a nice "round" number. It has a beginning, a middle, and an end. People can usually remember three things, so the concept of "three" has special meaning for speakers: three points, three solutions, three suggestions, three examples. Abraham Lincoln wrote "of the people, by the people, for the people"; Douglas MacArthur called on "duty, honor, country."

Following this concept, the rules for organizing a speech became amazingly simple. Just follow the old saying:

1. Tell what you're going to tell 'em.

2. Tell 'em.

3. Tell 'em what you just told 'em.

Now let's plug speech "jargon" into that simple outline:

1. Intro: Attention/opener and transition

2. Body: Expansion/points a, b, c and examples

3. Close: Summarize/final point/call to action

Many people tend to make speech organization too complicated. Even the longest presentation can be prepared using the above outline—it's simply a matter of increasing the number of examples, quotations, stories, and facts in each of the three sections.

Getting Started

Use a "web" or cluster chart to get started. Some people call these mind maps. The map can be simple or complicated, depending on your use for it, but it's always a great way to get the creative juices flowing, and especially in preparing a presentation. Mind mapping is a three-step process:

1. Write your topic in the center of a blank sheet of paper and draw a circle around it.

    Example: (Public Speaking)

2. Think of subpoints you think you'd like to include. Write them in the space around the main topic, draw circles around them, and then draw connecting lines from them to the main points they relate to.

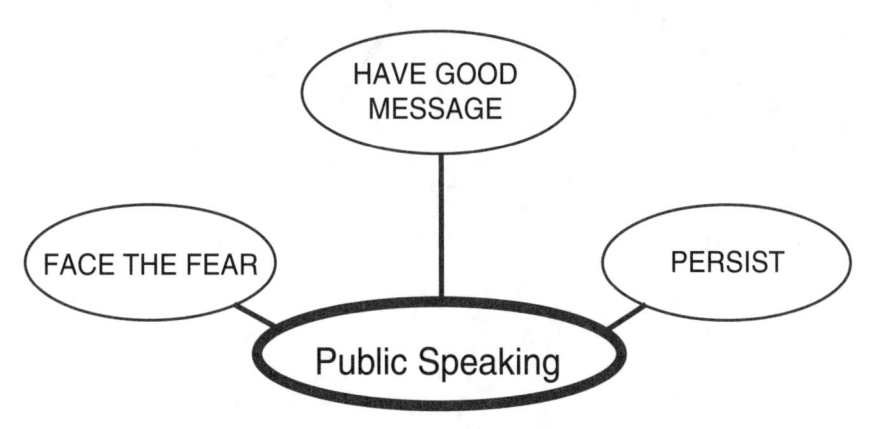

    HAVE GOOD MESSAGE
    FACE THE FEAR
    PERSIST
    Public Speaking

3. Keep adding ideas to those all over the page, drawing circles and connecting lines to keep the associations apparent to you. See page 78.

Writing Your Speech

Public Speaking

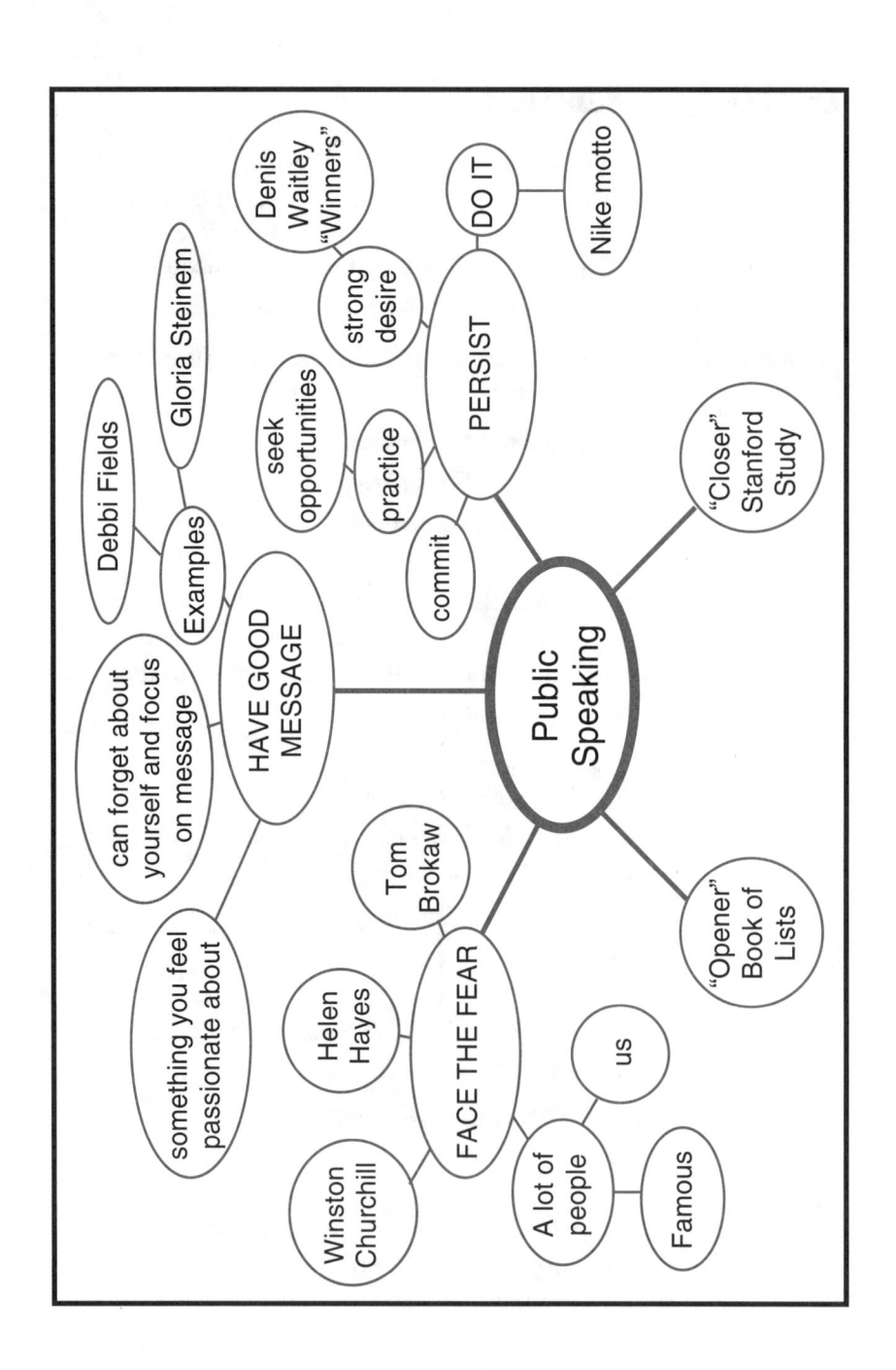

- **PERSIST**
  - DO IT — Nike motto
  - strong desire — Denis Waitley "Winners"
  - practice
  - seek opportunities
  - commit

- **HAVE GOOD MESSAGE**
  - Examples
    - Debbi Fields
    - Gloria Steinem
  - can forget about yourself and focus on message
  - something you feel passionate about

- **FACE THE FEAR**
  - Tom Brokaw
  - Helen Hayes
  - Winston Churchill
  - A lot of people
    - us
    - Famous

- "Closer" Stanford Study
- "Opener" Book of Lists

Speak Up and Stand Out

The process might seen messy and loose, but when you finish, you'll have created a general plan for what you'll talk about. In this visual rendition of your speech, you can see relationships (which is the advantage of webbing or clustering your points this way). You'll no doubt refine it, recopy it, and change it as you go. Some people get their cluster charts down to such a fine art, they use them as their notes for the presentation!

For those of you drawn to the trusty old outline, following is a typical, three-point presentation format. You may have only one point—that's fine! A short presentation just keeps everything short, narrowing the perspective and focusing on a basic idea. A longer speech or presentation can get into subpoints of subpoints, a little more complicated to plot as well as manage—just make sure everything really does relate.

> *"Never take any longer than absolutely necessary. The Ten Commandments are only 297 words. The Bill of Rights just 463. Lincoln's Gettysburg Address a mere 266. A single federal directive on the price of cabbage runs to 26,911 words."*
>
> —Aram Bakshian, Jr., editor,
> *American Speaker*

Writing Your Speech

[Title of presentation]
I. Introduction
   A. Opener (an attention-getting device)
   B. Importance of this topic
   C. Transition
II. Body
   A. Overview of main points
   B. Transition
      1. First point
         a) Story/anecdote/startling statistic/quote/etc.
         b) Your interpretation and information
         c) Transition
      2. Second point
         a) Story/anecdote/startling statistic/quote/etc.
         b) Your interpretation and information
         c) Transition
      3. Third point
         a) Story/anecdote/startling statistic/quote/etc.
         b) Your interpretation and information
         c) Transition
III. Conclusion
   A. Summary of all points
   B. Conclusion
   C. How/why the points all relate
   D. Importance
   E. Closer (the clincher, a device to bring informational and emotional closure)

Speak Up and Stand Out

Following is an example of a presentation plugged into the preceding outline format:

How to Succeed in Life: Public Speaking

I. Introduction

    A. Opener ("The Book of Lists says the fear of public speaking is the number one fear . . . above dying, fear of snakes, . . .")

    B. Importance of this topic ("In survey after survey, good communication is the number one business skill . . .")

    C. Transition ("So if this is both vital to our success as well as our greatest fear, then it seems important to feel the fear, and then do it anyway.")

II. Body

    A. Overview of main points ("I'd like to share three ideas with you. First, that a lot of famous people have faced their fear of public speaking; second, why they push themselves and overcome their fears; and third, what it takes to conquer the fear.")

    B. Transition ("Let's start with . . .")

        1. First point

            a) Story/anecdote/startling statistic/quote/etc. ("Winston Churchill fainted . . . , actress Helen Hayes had stage fright after sixty years on Broadway, Tom Brokaw overcame a speech impediment . . .")

            b) Your interpretation and information ("Many people famous and not have battled this malady and won . . .") .

Writing Your Speech

c) Transition ("How were they able to face their fear and win?")

2. Second point ("They wanted to. And they had something they wanted to say. Debbi Fields, of Mrs. Field's Cookies, said 'I made a resolution . . .' Gloria Steinem, high-profile feminist and political activist, said she was thirty years old before she ever spoke in public. . . . Everyone who battles the fear of public speaking does it because they have a message and ideas worth sharing.")

   a)

   b)

   c) Transition ("And how were they able to do it . . . ?")

3. Third point ("Persistence. Persistence. That's the way we learn any skill. You make a commitment and then practice, do it. Motivational speaker Dennis Waitley, who speaks about the psychology of winning, says that winners do what losers won't. Winners do what losers *don't* . . .")

   a)

   b)

   c) Transition ("If you know you could learn a skill that would increase your personal power, leadership potential, earning power, and self-esteem at the same time, would you be interested? How much would it be worth?")

III. Conclusion

    A. Summary of all points ("Yes, it's scary to stand in front of people and speak; we share that fear with many famous people. But they overcame it because they wanted to. How were they able to do it? The Nike motto is 'Just do it.' They just did it. They spoke again and again. That's persistence . . .")

    B. Conclusion ("We can too . . .")

    C. How/why the points all relate

    D. Importance ("Remember, public speaking is the number one skill needed in business today . . .")

    E. Closer ("According to a Stanford study, your success in life can be determined by the way you answer this question: Are you ready right now to stand up and give a speech?")

Openers and Closers: Powerful Start and Stop

Besides knowing the flow of the various parts of a presentation, it's important to understand their functions. The purpose of an opener is to immediately capture your listeners' attention and get the presentation off on the right track.

- It wakes them up.
- It makes them focus on the moment and the present situation.
- It pulls them up and out of any free-floating anxieties or thoughts.
- It sets the stage.

Writing Your Speech

- It makes the first impression.
- It creates interest for the rest of the message.

The purpose of the closer is to bring informational and emotional closure to your presentation. It can also do any or all of the following:

- It can charge your audience with a task or responsibility.
- It can remind your audience of the benefits.
- It can tell how they'll apply what you discussed.
- It can rephrase or summarize your key points.
- It can relate to current events or real-world situations.
- It can underline the importance of the topic.

Terri Sjodin, speaker and author of *SaleSpeak: Everybody Sells Something,* offers an interesting take on closing: "Most people conclude, but do not close. The close is what action you want your prospect (listener) to take as a result of your message. Remember to ask for the commitment; that is why you are there."

There are so many ways to open and/or close a presentation, you just have to be creative in thinking up possibilities and deciding which to use. Following are some ideas:

- Rhetorical question (a question you want your audience to answer to themselves)
- Current event tie-in (something in the news affecting the world, the country, or local concerns)
- Shocking statistic (a fact that is incredible, though true; be sure to attribute the source)
- Anecdote (story that illustrates a point)

- Relevant fact or statistics (not necessarily shocking, just informative)

- Scenario (paint a picture story; could end with the question, "What would you do?")

- Visual aid (a show and tell, a prop, a chart, a poster, a slide, etc.)

- Quotation (a saying from a recognized authority, or a saying that reflects insight)

The Body: The Mighty Middle

Arrange the points of your presentation so that your message has the most impact. Some topics almost dictate the approach, while others could be presented any number of ways. Some speakers fall into a rut and always present in one favorite way. However, the best conceived and most interesting presentations often take a different approach to a familiar topic. Here are some ideas on how to present your "middle" (the body of your talk):

- Chronologically (step 1, step 2; "First this happened, then . . .")

- The journalist's questions (who, what, when, where, why, and how)

- Most important to least important ("The number one biggest cause . . .")

- Least important to most important ("Three, two, and, ta da! Number ONE!")

- General to specific ("This is the general principle. . . . Here's an example . . .")

Writing Your Speech

- Specific to general ("Here are three examples . . .; from this we see a trend . . .")
- Compare and contrast ("With the old health plan . . . but now with the new . . .")
- Advantages and disadvantages (pros/cons, up side/down side)
- Cause and effect ("If you do/don't do . . . then this is what will occur . . .")
- Spatial (walking people through)

Transitions: The Smooth Connectors

In between your points, you'll need something to lead your listeners from one idea to another. A *transition* does just that: it moves things along. Transitions pull your audience through your material, point by point, linking ideas as you go. Following are some types of transitions:

- Summary of previous point ("We've been talking about . . .; now let's move to . . .")
- Preview of next point ("What we'll talk about next is . . .")
- Comparison/contrast ("The original blueprint has this approach; the new one looks at it differently. . . .")
- Sequence/order ("We've covered three points so far, now here's number four. . . .")
- Consequence/result ("And so we see when . . . is done/called/neglected/implemented, then . . . happens.")

Speak Up and Stand Out

Support Material

Support materials for the substance of your presentation can come from many sources. Here are some examples to get you started:

- Magazines, newspapers, books
- Computer search services
- On-line computer networks
- Libraries, reference librarians
- Your organization's files, scrapbooks
- Media reports and documentaries
- Information specialists, researchers
- Your professional/personal notes, files
- Your own life experience

With regard to the last item, ask yourself what unique perspective you can offer the audience. Is there something in your life, your personal and professional experience that is worth sharing here? Veteran speakers have often found that the things people remember from their presentations are the "up close and personal" stories.

So, here's the challenge: Look for presentation examples and stories in your everyday life. It's just a matter of stopping, looking, thinking, connecting, relating, and recording, and then telling it conversationally. Sound simple? It's not, but it's worth it. *The more personal you are, the more universal you are.* Nineteenth-century American writers Henry David Thoreau and Walt Whitman wrote about the value of life's little moments. Robert Fulghum, author of *All I Needed to Know I Learned in Kindergarten* and *Uh-Oh: Some Observations From Both Sides of*

Writing Your Speech

the Refrigerator Door, knows how to discover the extraordinary in ordinary events. He describes a midnight peanut butter and jelly snack in mystical terms, and turns kindergarten into a pivotal learning experience.

Here's a synopsis of the kinds of stories to consider including in your presentations:

- Ha Ha! (funny)
- Aha! (surprise, mystery, clever)
- Ah! (love, cute)
- Amen! (I understand, I agree)

Add Humor and Vitality

Getting your audience to laugh is one of the fastest and more effective ways to establish rapport and create a warm, responsive atmosphere. And listen up: even if your basic information is serious or technical, you can use humor to introduce, explain, transition, and summarize!

In his book *Using Humor for Effective Business Speaking,* Gene Perret asserts that the more serious the topic, the more likely it is to be categorized as "pompous." He says that it's the speaker's obligation to keep the audience's attention. The best way to do that, he says, is to balance the presentation with humor.

Humor creates interest and attention. It makes the speaker appear more human and gets the audience into his or her camp. When a speaker stands before an audience, The Great Divide may lag between them. That is, people may be physically present but mentally or emotionally preoccupied. The sooner you get people to laugh with you, the faster you close the distance.

Speak Up and Stand Out

When an audience is laughing out loud, even just chuckling or smiling with you, The Great Divide starts to shrink. You become one with the group and can take them into your topic and emotional state.

In addition, humor enhances high information retention. It makes people remember more. Humor creates a positive, funny, emotional experience (right brain) around the information processing (left brain). Imagine the impact you can have on your audience if you are keeping each participant's whole brain busy!

Many books have been written on the subject of humor and what makes something funny. It can be a science or an art, or both. Professional comedians know that humor is a combination of style, word selection, sounds and vocal inflection, distinctive delivery, the perfect pause, and the right mixture of gestures and body language.

Professional comic actors and comedians each have a certain style. And you can believe they've worked hard to find what works for them. Which is what you need to do: find what works for you. A personal style of humor settles in when you begin to let it be you. Imitating someone else can get you started, but won't hold forever. You only find out by trying something and welcoming the resulting feedback.

To find your personal style of humor:

- Inject humor in your presentations, on purpose. (You can't just hope it happens.) Actively hunt for humorous ideas to strategically place in your presentations.

- Listen to your feedback (fans who come up and chat; participants who give you written evaluations).

- Get a coach or hire a professional humor/speech consultant.

Writing Your Speech

- Ask a trusted colleague to listen, observe the audience, and take notes on anything that gets even a snicker.
- Take an acting or comedy class and see what comes naturally.
- Introduce more of what seems to work for you—one-liners, jokes, personal stories and experiences, personal asides, ad libs, word choices, inflection, changes in pitch or pace, facial expressions, body reactions, and so on.

Where does the material come from?

- Create a humor file. Keep news stories, editorials, cartoons, and so forth that show the lighter and nonsensical side of life.
- Listen to others. When people share the humorous, ironic, or crazy things that happen to them, write them down.
- Keep a journal of the funny things that happen to you too.

What kinds of humor might work in your presentation?

- People (their foibles)
- The human condition (incidents that seem odd, nonsensical, or ironic)
- Obvious overstatement and exaggeration
- Puns/double meanings
- Language that is obviously pedantic, alliterative, or wordy
- Surprises (leading the audience to think you'll say the usual thing but saying just the opposite, or something different)
- Irony (saying something in a manner that shows you mean the exact opposite)
- Poking fun at authority

Speak Up and Stand Out

- Silliness (treating absurd things seriously or serious things absurdly)
- Voice changes (pitch, pace, especially when it's unexpected)
- Gestures and body language

What to Call It

Finally, though this may seem backward to you, consider choosing a title for your presentation last. The advantage in doing so comes from your familiarity and understanding at that point. As with every other aspect of your preparation, there are a few pointers to keep in mind here:

- Keep the title short. Consider how it will look in the program.
- Be sure it really says what you're going to talk about.
- Make it interest-grabbing for the particular group.
- Make it catchy. Toy with words and try to come up with something that has a nice "ring" to it. Consider alliteration or a play on words.
- Be sure the mood of the title sets the tone for the speech.
- Say the title aloud and "see" how it sounds.
- Bounce it off a few people you trust to get their reactions.
- Think of the title as a one-sentence summary or the essence of your entire speech.

Writing Your Speech

The Ten Commandments of Humor in Presentations

1. Humor should be relevant to your subject. It should move your message forward, not take the audience's attention away from the subject.

2. Humor should be in good taste. When in doubt, leave it out.

3. Make the story sound like it really happened—even if it didn't.

4. Personalize the story. Instead of telling about someone else in an airport or the pet store, make it you or the power person in the audience (if you decide they won't mind).

5. Localize the humor. Tell the story as if it happened in the place and town where you are.

6. Sprinkle humor at intervals throughout the speech. Humor keeps people alert and awake.

7. Know your stories backward and forward, so you can tell them easily without stumbling.

8. Know what you're up against. People's receptivity to humor increases as the day goes on. Breakfast time is tough, lunch is better, dinner is even better. And after dinner is best.

9. Don't announce a funny story. Just tell it. If the audience laughs, it was a funny story. If they don't, it was just a story.

10. Laugh at yourself. People like speakers who do not take themselves too seriously. This allows the audience to momentarily feel equal, or even superior. Note, though, that this sort of self-put-down only works if you are clearly confident.

nine

Choosing Audiovisual Aids

Q. *Why have a "dog and pony" show?*

A. *Two great reasons: attention and retention.*

The "how to" guide of the 3M Corporation says that when we rely on words alone to communicate, "an estimated 90 percent of a message is misinterpreted or forgotten entirely. We retain only 10 percent of what we hear. Adding appropriate visual aids to verbalization increases retention to approximately 50 percent."

Why is this so?

- **AV aids help people get the information.** Some people process information best aurally (hearing it), others process it best visually (seeing it), and still others process it better if they *do* something (kinesthetics). The majority of people are "visually" oriented, which means anything you can do to bring something to your presentation for the audience to look at is going to work for the majority.

- **AV aids make you more persuasive in less time.** According to Raines and Williamson in *Using Visual Aids,* presenters using visuals conduct meetings in 28 percent less time, increase audience retention as much as five times, and get proposals approved twice as often.

- **AV aids add variety and emphasis to your presentation.** It's not just kids who have a short attention span. In this video age, people seem to have an imaginary remote control if something is not holding their attention.

Speak Up and Stand Out

They'll switch you off mentally (by thinking of other things, reading, chatting) or physically (they'll leave!). To give you an idea how technology has changed our attention span, consider the changes in television production. *The Honeymooners* was shot with one camera, *Bonanza* with six. In *Miami Vice,* the camera angles changed every six seconds, and on MTV, they change every one and a half seconds!

- **AV aids help you organize your presentation.** In the process of preparation, you are forced to sequence the material you present. This clarifies your ideas and orders them in a logical manner.

- **AV aids help you to be clear and concise.** As you are sequencing and deciding on the content of your visual aids, the process forces you to distill and refine your ideas.

Bottom line on AV aids: use them to clarify an idea, emphasize a point, add variety to your presentation, enhance your professional image, record the proceedings, and bring your audience along with you. Most importantly, though, remember that *you* are your best visual aid.

In fact, you are the *number one* visual aid. Since more than half of communications is body language, you cannot afford to take this lightly. It also means you'll want to make a special effort to be seen by each member of your audience. Part of your preparation should include the following important questions:

- Will I need a platform?
- How's the lighting? Do I need a spotlight on me?
- Will I walk around and/or into the audience?
- Where do I need to stand to be seen by all and for maximum impact?

Choosing Audiovisual Aids

Remember that however you present yourself and whatever else you bring in for your audience to see should enhance your message, not detract or distract. Visuals should not upstage you or your message.

Following are some pros and cons of various AV options.

Chalkboard and Whiteboard

Advantages:

- Traditional visual tool for training
- Best for small groups (twenty-five or fewer)
- Easy to write key points and words
- Easy to add and refer to responses from the audience
- Easy to erase and reuse immediately
- Relatively available and inexpensive
- Chalk and markers easy to transport
- Electronic versions allow creation of paper copies of drawings and notes

Disadvantages:

- Not effective with large groups
- Speaker must turn back to write
- Sometimes difficult to position so that all can see
- Repeated chalk erasures can leave the surface cloudy
- Must write large enough for all to see

Tips for using chalkboard or whiteboard:

- Write large enough for the back row to see (two-inch letters for viewing up to thirty feet away).

- Simple, block printing is best, in upper- and lowercase.
- Limit writing to key phrases or words.
- Go for contrast:
  - Black chalkboards with white chalk are more legible than green boards.
  - Black markers on whiteboards are most legible; next is navy, then dark green. Watch out for yellow—it tends to disappear.
  - Use different colors for emphasis and variety, but be sure they can be seen.
- Use a pointer rather than your hand so you can stand a distance away.
- Use a chalk holder to minimize chalk dust on your hands and clothes.
- Focus the audience on a key phrase by erasing the rest of the board.
- For greater flexibility, use two boards on separate easels.
- Erase the entire board or remove it when you are finished so the audience is not distracted.
- If you are using the board repeatedly, have a damp cloth (for chalkboards) or liquid eraser (for whiteboards) on hand to ensure good legibility.
- If you prewrite some information, keep the board turned around or hidden until you want the audience to see it, or they'll be reading it before you want them to.

Choosing Audiovisual Aids

Flip Charts

Advantages:

- Relatively inexpensive
- Can be prepared in advance
- Can use color in drawings, letters, graphs, and charts
- Best for small groups (less than thirty in theater seating)
- Tend to be rather informal
- Can list and refer to responses from audience
- Can tear off and tape on walls to keep record of information
- Can be folded up and retained for future reference
- Come in unlined, lined, or grid paper

Disadvantages:

- Not effective with large groups (more than thirty to forty in theater seating)
- Must carefully seat everyone so they can see chart
- Can lose audience interest if back is turned for too long
- Requires decent to excellent handwriting

Tips for using flip charts:

- Legibility is always a key factor, so make sure your letters are thick and large enough (two-inch-high minimum).
- Practice turning the sheets until the action becomes easy and smooth.
- Using sheets with very light grid marks makes it easy to keep lines straight.

- Limit your writing to key phrases or words.
- Face your audience as much as possible.
- Use a pointer rather than your hand to indicate details or specific words.
- Step away from the flip chart when you're not writing so you don't block the audience's view.
- If you'll be referring to one particular sheet more than once, make it easy to locate by placing a tab on it.
- Lightly pencil in the outline of an illustration you want to "draw" during your presentation.
- On a corner of the page, lightly pencil in the main points you want to cover on that sheet.
- Black markers are the best for contrast and legibility.
- Watch for bleeding through (permanent and dark markers tend to do this).
- Use colored markers for variety and added touches.
- Draw a simple border on each page to unify the flip chart sheets.
- When carrying the flip chart, use a bungee cord to keep the pages together.

Posters

Advantages:

- Can be prepared in advance
- Stiff paper has a finished look
- Tend to be informal, depending on the quality and style of artwork

Choosing Audiovisual Aids

- Can be used to show a prop or piece of equipment that would be too difficult to bring along
- Can be kept, even laminated, and posted in key areas for high visibility
- Inexpensive and materials are readily available

Disadvantages:

- Somewhat difficult to keep from getting tattered with use
- Effective for relatively small groups (up to thirty in theater seating)
- Can be too expensive and bulky to use multiple sheets for writing on-the-spot notes and responses from the audience
- Require an easel to display and more difficult to attach to the wall
- Take time, effort, and some talent to do well

Tips for using posters:

- Position the poster on a stationary easel for best visibility.
- Large, thick letters are the key (two-inch-high minimum).
- Posters should be well done—nothing shoddy works in this medium.
- Use a pointer rather than your hands so you can stand a distance away.
- If you have several posters to display during your presentation, practice changing them so you look smooth and organized.
- White paper is still the best; bright colors tend to overpower your message.

- Use color and contrasting pens.
- Simplify drawings, using symbols and abbreviations where appropriate.
- If you're using many posters and will be referring often to one in particular, mark it with a tab so you can locate it quickly.
- If you want to draw or write something during a presentation but want to do a good job quickly, lightly pencil it in place beforehand.
- Lamination preserves your posters.

Overhead Projector/ Transparencies

Advantages:

- No need to darken the room
- Can be used for small to large groups (up to two hundred in a well-arranged room)
- Very common piece of equipment at hotels, businesses, and organizations
- Relatively low tech, not many moving parts and with proper care can last for years
- Transparencies (also called *foils* or *cels*) and supplies are relatively inexpensive
- Transparencies easily portable
- Transparencies easy to arrange, access, and change
- Speaker can face the group at all times
- Speaker can maintain complete control

Choosing Audiovisual Aids

- Easy to use a pen or pointer on the projector itself
- Can be used periodically during presentation with flip of switch
- Can reveal information one word or line at a time
- Allows highlighting and personalizing during presentation
- Allows recording immediate feedback from audience, projected for whole group to see
- Can be created with readily available supplies
- Can reuse sheets
- Can accommodate horizontal or vertical format
- Can use the transparency frame for notes
- Can be simple or fancy, with or without color and graphics
- New technology: feeders that move your next transparency in place by remote control

Disadvantages:

- Keystone effect of image is possible unless projector and screen are carefully positioned or freestanding screen has a metal extender to bring top of screen closer to projector than bottom

"Have your presentation in a variety of formats. Mine is in print, overheads, 33mm slides, and on my computer. That way no matter what happens to the equipment, or if the audience is larger/smaller than expected, I can adjust and use the appropriate visual."

—Sharon Adcock, speaker/trainer

- Furnished projector may be anything from adequate to awful
- Ensuring that each group member can see can be a challenge
- Can become monotonous if used throughout an entire and lengthy presentation
- Projected image not as good as a slide
- Distracting noise from motor and fan

Tips for using an overhead projector:

- Position the screen and projector for the largest, clearest image possible.
- Position it so you can easily use it and the audience can easily see it.
- Use colored pens and cels for good effect.
- Use overlays for showing the parts of a whole.
- Cover some of the message and reveal a line at a time.
- Use a transparency frame or use masking tape on the glass surface of the projector to block off the area of the cel you want to show.
- Turn the light off while changing transparencies, or use a sheet of cardboard to cover the top lens and mirror.
- Practice your changes and motions before you present.
- Place the transparency in position before you turn the light on.
- Choreograph your motions to turn the light on at the very moment you want to emphasize the information on the screen.

Choosing Audiovisual Aids

- Know how to change the bulb and where to find a spare.
- Use the rule of 6 by 6 to design each transparency for maximum readability—six words per line and six lines per page.
- Use font styles and sizes that are easy to read. Big, bold, and clear is what you're looking for.
- Don't block the view of the screen with your body; move as needed.
- Don't use old, faded pens.
- Don't leave the light on with no transparency showing.
- Don't present complicated or confusing designs, or those that are small or contain too much print.
- Don't use a vertical format too often—it's more difficult to read.
- Don't switch frequently from horizontal to vertical format because it interrupts the flow.

Slides

Advantages:

- Can be used for small to very large audiences (up to six hundred people)
- Equipment operates with a push of a button (with carousel projector and remote control)
- Specific areas can be isolated with use of a laser pointer

- Flexible format
  - Can dwell on one slide as long as desired
  - One step, one motion turns the image on
  - Can move forward or backward in presentation
  - Can be changed and reordered to customize and update a presentation
- Photos reproduce well on slides
- Color graphics give an authoritative image
- Offers a professional, polished image

Disadvantages:

- Room must be darkened for maximum effect (limits eye contact, limits ability to read audience reactions, contributes to drowsiness)
- More planning and preparation needed to have slides ready
- Can't alter or write on slides during presentation
- Carousels bulky for transporting
- More movable parts means more can go wrong (slides can jam, remote control can break, bulb can burn out, etc.)

Tips for using a 35-mm slide projector:

- Use cardboard frames on slides; plastic ones can warp when they get hot.
- Be sure the slides are loaded properly (i.e., all facing the proper direction).
- Choose only the best, high-quality slides.

- Stand to the right of the screen, facing the audience. That's a strong position. Since the audience reads from left to right, you will be in their line of sight at the beginning of every slide.
- Check all cords and quickly run through your slides prior to your presentation.
- Memorize what you'll say during the slide portion because there is less light and you'll want to keep your attention on the flow of information.
- Remember to change slides often enough to keep the audience attention focused.
    - *Quick change:* six to ten seconds each
    - *Moderate change:* ten to twenty seconds each
    - *Slow changes for more detailed explanation:* one or two minutes
- Stick with one format (horizontal or vertical) throughout.
- Design your slides for the last row of your audience; limit the number of words per line and lines per slide.
- Carefully number and label your slides for each presentation so they can be reordered in case of a mixup.
- Mark one corner of each slide as it is in place in the carousel or slide tray, ready to present. You can see at a glance if all slides are in position (not backward or upside down).
- Mark the remote control with tape so you can tell by touch which is the "forward" button.

Audiotapes

Advantages:

- Easy to use
- Available and inexpensive
- Easy to produce
- Easy to carry, even with the tape player
- Music can set or change a mood
- Prerecorded statements/dialogue can underline a point or spark discussion
- Other voices and experts become readily "available"

Disadvantages:

- Must be loud enough for all to hear
- Must cue up (or have separate tapes for each audio segment)

Tips for using an audiotape recorder:

- Cue up tapes so they're ready to go.
- Have volume already adjusted for the size of the room and your group.
- Experiment with ways to make your presentations "sparkle" with extra sound.

Videotapes

Advantages:

- TV monitor can be used in lighted room
- Easy to use straight through and to stop for discussions

Choosing Audiovisual Aids

- Show motion and closeups
- Screen titling and "fancier" transitions possible between scenes
- Equipment (camera and editing capabilities) continues to become more affordable
- TV monitors/VCR equipment easily available
- Videotape easy to transport
- Sound, sight, and scene changes very powerful in creating emotions
- Can standardize training or information updates for many employees or groups

Disadvantages:

- Monitors not big enough for large groups
- Renting a large screen, multiple receivers, or rear view projection equipment is expensive and not available in all facilities or cities
- Audio can suffer because of small amplifiers and speakers in TV sets
- Amateur videos can detract from message (TV-age audiences have a high level of expectation from this medium)

Tips for using videotapes:

- With groups of more than thirty or forty, use more than one TV monitor.
- Give a good introduction to the videotape.

- Cue up the tape, so it's ready to go. Push the play button and increase the volume as needed. (Avoid an "audio attack" from sound that's set too loud!)
- Ensure proper amplification so that all members of the audience can hear (may involve extra speakers).
- Keep audio segments short, because an audience will tend to lose interest with sound coming from a separate source (not you).

Multimedia

Advantages:

- Dazzling features create high visual interest
- Easy to edit, update, change
- Different combinations of equipment, so size and bulkiness vary
- Impresses audiences

Disadvantages:

- Expensive to own or rent equipment
- Probably need to furnish your own equipment for most settings
- Portability a challenge
- Need to darken the room
- Need to know not only how to use equipment, but all about setup and troubleshooting
- Overreliance on "bells and whistles"

Choosing Audiovisual Aids

Props and Objects

Advantages:

- Models, objects add realism to a presentation
- Things that wiggle or move are especially interesting
- 3-D aspect offers distinct advantage over pictures
- Can be handled and passed around among the participants, giving a kinesthetic dimension to presentation
- Weird, unusual items can add humor

Disadvantages:

- Models and objects not as effective with large groups (unless they are huge)
- Can be unwieldy to transport

Handouts

Advantages:

- Overview of what the presentation will cover
- Something to follow along with
- A place to take notes
- Something to take home
- Professional-looking materials enhance speaker's image
- Moves things along faster
- Keeps speaker on track
- Timing of distribution helps control audience attentiveness
- Broad price range
- Can double as promotion piece

Disadvantages:

- Prevent/inhibit skipping around
- Add noise (rustling of papers)
- Encourage reading ahead, previewing material
- "Perfect" format elusive (some users like to take notes, others want it all there)

Pointers

When using any visual aids, look like a professional: use a pointer! There are several products made and marketed for the express purpose of use in presentations.

- **Laser pointer:** Looks like a fat fountain pen. Handy to carry and use, it projects a laser point of light on the wall or screen. These are pressure sensitive, so the light is only on when you purposely point.
- **Collapsible pointer:** Looks like a pen when fully collapsed, like car radio antenna when extended. These usually extend to approximately twenty-four inches.
- **Wooden pointer with black rubber tip:** Approximately thirty to forty inches long.
- **Creative pointers:** Variety available, especially for use with overhead projectors (e.g., translucent plastic pointers in bright colors). You can also create your own, using swizzle sticks or cardboard. Even using a pen or pencil is better than using your hand or fingers because it is a hard, stiff extension and keeps your body away from your information so the audience can see.

Equipment Failure

Whether equipment failure is disastrous or merely inconvenient depends on how important the equipment (that is, the visual aids it supports) is to your presentation. If a breakdown would spell catastrophe, then *definitely* have a Plan B ready to roll out of the wings (such as a second slide projector that you can just pop your carousel into). For failures of the typical variety (i.e., temporary and fixable), following are some tips to ride them out:

- Call for a short break.
- Move on with another part of the presentation while the equipment is being fixed.
- Take questions while the equipment is being fixed or replaced.
- If the repair/replacement is going to be disruptive or distracting, wait until the break to start.
- Be prepared to deal with this—it's one of Murphy's favorites!

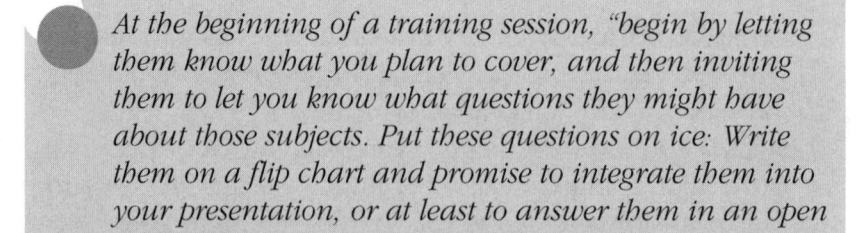

> *At the beginning of a training session, "begin by letting them know what you plan to cover, and then inviting them to let you know what questions they might have about those subjects. Put these questions on ice: Write them on a flip chart and promise to integrate them into your presentation, or at least to answer them in an open forum before the end of the day."*
>
> —Frank O'Meara, "The Pedagogue's Decalogue," *Training Magazine*

ten

Creating Your Environment

Q. *What about room setup, lecterns, and microphones?*

A. *Glad you asked. The physical arrangement also speaks volumes about you as a speaker and can also influence how well the audience receives and accepts your message.*

As members of the audience enter the presentation room, they are already forming an impression of what the experience is going to be like. The environment creates an impression and evokes a reaction. Think of it: the building, the room, the size of the room, the colors, the carpeting, the height of the ceiling, the lighting, the chairs, the placement of the chairs, plain tables, tables with tablecloths, a stage or risers, evidence of audiovisual equipment, how much/how little space there is. In other words, surroundings add up to create a response in the listener-to-be!

If the facilities, room, or setup could talk, it might say something like the following:

- I'm ready.
- I'm clean.
- I'm well used, but well cared for.
- I'm set up for this event, but we had to hurry—sorry about the leftover trash by the chairs.
- I'm set up for classroom learning, with rows of tables.

Speak Up and Stand Out

- I'm set up for togetherness, with the chairs touching.
- I'm set up for participation, with the chairs set in curving rows.
- I'm set up so everyone can see the speaker.
- I'm set up to create an atmosphere.
- I'm set up to focus on images projected on a screen.
- I'm set up for more people than the speaker anticipated.
- I'm so big I can seat hundreds; however, only ten people are coming.
- I'm set up by people who are used to taking care of every little detail.

Suit the Seating Arrangement to the Occasion

Following are some typical seating arrangements used by presenters. Each one has advantages and disadvantages, according to the occasion and the type of atmosphere you want to create. In the diagrams that follow, an "X" represents the arrangement's main focus; an "x" equals additional focus.

Creating Your Environment

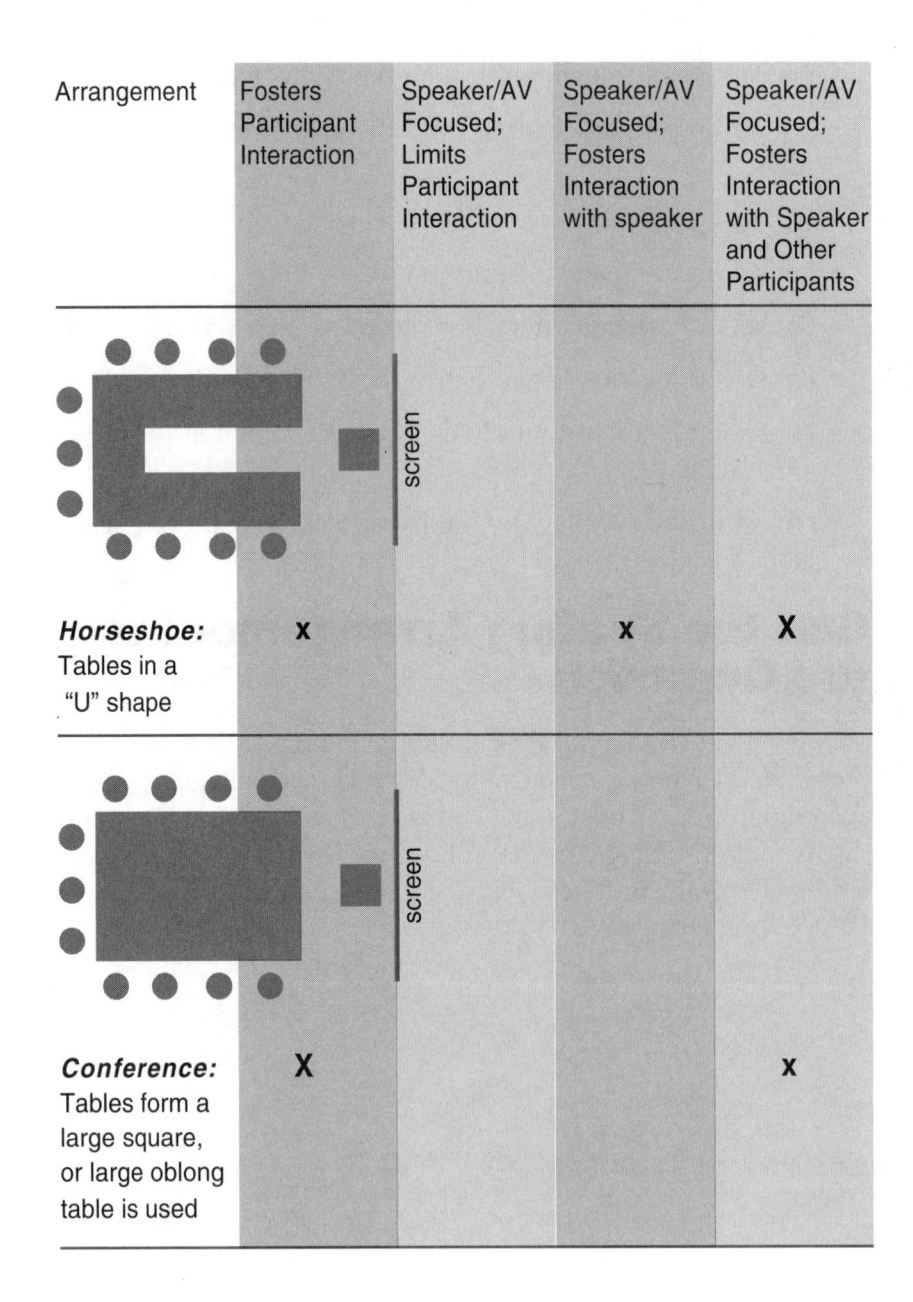

Arrangement	Fosters Participant Interaction	Speaker/AV Focused; Limits Participant Interaction	Speaker/AV Focused; Fosters Interaction with speaker	Speaker/AV Focused; Fosters Interaction with Speaker and Other Participants
Horseshoe: Tables in a "U" shape	X		X	X
Conference: Tables form a large square, or large oblong table is used	X			X

Speak Up and Stand Out

Arrangement	Fosters Participant Interaction	Speaker/AV Focused; Limits Participant Interaction	Speaker/AV Focused; Fosters Interaction with speaker	Speaker/AV Focused; Fosters Interaction with Speaker and Other Participants
Banquet: Round tables	X		x	X
Classroom: Tables in rows		x	X	

Creating Your Environment

Arrangement	Fosters Participant Interaction	Speaker/AV Focused; Limits Participant Interaction	Speaker/AV Focused; Fosters Interaction with speaker	Speaker/AV Focused; Fosters Interaction with Speaker and Other Participants
Classroom: "chevron" style			X	x
Theatre: Straight rows of chairs	x		X	

Speak Up and Stand Out

Arrangement	Fosters Participant Interaction	Speaker/AV Focused; Limits Participant Interaction	Speaker/AV Focused; Fosters Interaction with speaker	Speaker/AV Focused; Fosters Interaction with Speaker and Other Participants
Theatre: Curved rows of chairs	x		x	x

> "Details don't mean a lot—they mean everything. When I give a speech, I carry a roll of masking tape with me. Whoever designed ballroom doors obviously never had to give a speech. When they close, there's a bang that takes everybody out of the speech. So I tape the latches, and the doors close silently."
>
> —Harvey Mackay, *Swim with the Sharks*

Creating Your Environment

Arranging and Using Other Room Items

Following are descriptions of other items you'll encounter and plan for in the room's physical environment:

- **Lectern.** This is a reading stand, used to hold notes. Often freestanding, it usually comes up to about elbow height on most speakers. Frequently there's a microphone attached, and some have extra amenities such as a reading light, a clock, or a light system that alerts speakers of time limits. This piece of furniture is often incorrectly called a *podium*.

  Walk out from behind the lectern, even if one is provided. The lectern presents a physical barrier, which can create a psychological barrier. Also, you'll look more confident and professional.

- **Dais (DAY-us).** This raised platform is commonly used to seat "dignitaries," a panel of speakers, and so on. They come in various sizes to accommodate different arrangements such as table(s) and chairs, lectern and side chairs, a screen for projected images, and so forth.

- **Microphone.** In general, a microphone (voice amplifier) is not something to be afraid of; it's designed to help you, to ensure that your listeners have no trouble hearing you. A normal voice is all you need—the microphone will handle the amplification.

  Under normal conditions for most speakers, the standard microphone arrangements are as follows:

  - On a stand or at the lectern (limited flexibility; sometimes mike on a gooseneck, which can be twisted so you can stand beside the lectern)

Speak Up and Stand Out

- Hand-held, with long cord (creates a "tail"—guard against tripping over it or wrapping it around a table; limited distance for speaker movement)
- Hand-held, wireless (lots of freedom to move around room or stage; one hand constantly busy holding mike, leaving only one hand for gestures)
- Lavaliere type, attached to long cord in wall system (clips to tie, lapel, etc.; again, creates a tail, but leaves hands free)
- Lavaliere type, wireless (clips to clothes; has short cord leading to a transmitter pack that clips to waistline, concealed from view; has off/on switch; the ultimate in speaker freedom)

There are some tips you should observe for using a microphone effectively:

- Check the mike before you speak—before the event begins.
- Check for volume control. Have someone set it after checking for proper volume from the back of the room.
- Test the mike in your normal voice, then test a sentence from the loudest, most intense section of your presentation, and then the softest part too.
- Adjust a standing mike for appropriate height; set it just below your chin.
- Know where the on/off switch is, and make sure it's on when you start.
- Keep stand or hand-held mikes about six inches from your face, and turn at a forty-five-degree angle so you can talk across the front rather than directly into it. This will help avoid "popping p's" and "hissing s's."

Creating Your Environment

- Step back or pull the mike away if you want to speak louder than normal; get closer or pull the mike closer to your mouth if you want to speak softly or whisper.
- Observe those who use the mike before you do, and benefit from their experience.
- Do use a mike, if a good system is available. You can talk in a normal voice and not have to project and distort your voice trying to make sure people hear.
- Don't blow into a mike or thump on it to test it.
- Don't shout into a mike; if you're going to increase your volume, stand back for that part.
- Don't fiddle with the mike after you have started your presentation.
- Don't cover your face with the mike—you don't want to look like you're eating it!
- Don't talk too fast, or too loud, or put your mouth too close to the mike.
- Don't worry about the mike; keep your mind on your audience and your message.
- Don't expect the mike to demonstrate vocal variety; you'll have to create that, with your change of pace and pitch, inflection, and emphasis.

> "Bright lights increase the energy in the room and make the audience and the speaker more alert."
>
> —Elizabeth Jeffries, *The Heart of Leadership: Influencing by Design*

Speak Up and Stand Out

Fire Drills, Lights Out, and Other Interruptions

Occasionally your speaking environment will spring a surprise on you in the form of a power failure or similar disruption. In such a situation, you are the leader the audience will look to. Here are some tips for handling these situations:

- Don't panic; yours should be the reassuring voice.

- Follow orders from the facility representatives if they ask everyone to evacuate the building.

- Lights out? Use your sense of humor. If you're in the dark for more than fifteen seconds, send someone to see what's going on. You may have to take a break.

- If your format makes it feasible, you may want to move the group outside. In cases where an emergency light illuminates the room at least somewhat, use the time for a question-and-answer session.

> *"There's always something you can't control. It's the way you react to a glitch that the audience will remember. If you handle it with balance and a sense of humor, they will appreciate it."*
>
> —Nancy Austin, speaker/co-author,
> *A Passion for Excellence*

Creating Your Environment

eleven

Handling Special Speaking Opportunities

Q. *Do I need specific preparation for special speaking situations?*

A. *Not necessarily—you can stretch the basic principles to fit.*

Up to this point, we've been examining and preparing for fairly standard and/or scheduled-in-advance types of presentations. But as you've probably observed or experienced firsthand, this doesn't describe the whole arena of public speaking. There will be times when you may be asked to speak on the spur of the moment to a group, or perhaps you'll be invited to give an interview—a very different set of dynamics for making a personal presentation.

What you will discover is that you have the foundation in place to rise to these special occasions.

"Extemporaneous" or "Impromptu" Speeches

Extemporaneous speaking (from the Latin "out of time") refers to improvised, unpremeditated, offhand presentations, those composed and performed on the spur of the moment, for example:

- You are in a staff meeting and someone asks you several questions about a project. You did not anticipate the subject would even come up, let alone that you would be asked to "report."

Speak Up and Stand Out

- You are on your break and a co-worker asks you to explain how the health plan deductible works. You have limited knowledge, but share what you know.

- You are in a class or conference and the speaker refers to you as a person who has had experience with "that kind of thing." You are asked to stand and describe how you or your office staff handled it.

Impromptu speeches (also from Latin, meaning "in readiness") occur with little preparation or without previous study, preparation, or consideration, for example:

- You are gathered for a staff meeting and right before it starts, the team leader unexpectedly asks you to be ready to give a five-minute report on the upcoming regional meeting, which you have been organizing.

- You were away from your desk when an upset client phoned. Your secretary took the message, and now you must collect your thoughts, facts, and emotions and return the call.

- You have attended a breakfast meeting of your professional organization. The chair comes to you in a panic because the speaker just called in sick—would you please take twenty minutes on any topic of your choice, something you think the crowd needs or just something of interest on your mind?

There's a subtle difference between extemporaneous and impromptu speaking, and it lies in the expected immediacy of the response. With impromptu, you have a moment, maybe even a few moments, to collect your thoughts and organize some ideas.

When they suddenly ask you to "say a few words . . ."

- Quickly decide what you want to comment on.
- Think of your objective: to inform, motivate, persuade, or entertain?
- Jot down your simple organizational method and fill it in:
  - Intro (general remarks, a good opener you've done before that gets you into your topic)
  - Closing (review statement, summary remarks)
  - Body (limit yourself to a few key points—three if you have them, two is fine, and even one *good* point is excellent; state your point or points to your audience up front)
- Proceed with your remarks (without belaboring the "suddenness of this assignment").
- Open a Q&A session if time and format permit:
  - Move toward the audience.
  - Raise your own hand as you ask for questions.
  - Ask open-ended questions, wait for a response, and then answer with your own views if no one volunteers. Ask for comments on the viewpoint you gave.
  - Choose someone from the audience who's been an active listener, or participated earlier, and ask that person a direct question.
  - Have some questions in mind. Say, "Sometimes I get asked the question . . ." or "Is anybody wondering why . . ." (and then answer it).

Speak Up and Stand Out

Effective Media Interviews

A "live" media interview is the perfect situation to see how your public speaking skills all come together. This is the time to demonstrate:

- Your facility with language.
- Your knowledge of your subject.
- Your preparation.
- Your energy and enthusiasm for your message.

This opportunity is related to *impromptu* speaking in that you need to be "in readiness." That is, you know your topic—you just don't know the questions. There is an element of surprise involved.

In general:

- Get to know your interviewer if possible. At least try to listen to the station, look at the program, and/or read the publication. This does make a difference as you psychologically prepare.
- Decide on a basic message, a major point you want to make.
- Make your main points early in the interview.
- Have your stories, facts and stats, opinions, and quotations ready to share.
- Rehearse your statements to a friendly wall, or let a trusted colleague ask you questions from a list you've prepared.
- Let your interviewer have a copy of your well-thought out questions.

Handling Special Speaking Opportunities

- Keep your message conversational. This is a one-on-one experience—the audience will usually be listening or reading one at a time.

- Ask ahead of time about receiving a copy of the interview. Provide audio or videocassettes, or arrange to tape it yourself. For print copies, it's always a good plan to furnish a self-addressed stamped envelope. Make the process easy for the interviewer.

- Send a thank you note after the interview.

When you're being interviewed in person:

- Arrive early. Nothing is worse than doing an interview when you're feeling hassled and rushed.

- Be a friend. Greet your interviewer as you would a valued customer.

- Keep your answers short and to the point. Listeners and interviewers like that; plus, if this interview will be edited, you'll have a better chance of being quoted correctly.

- Use the inverted pyramid principle. Start with the most important information first; then build on it with facts, examples, and anecdotes.

- For short interviews, have one to four main points. For longer interviews, have the same number of points, but be ready with more examples and anecdotes to support them.

- Answer questions honestly. Don't make it sound like you have something to hide. Evasiveness or equivocation is out.

- Think of each question as an opportunity to respond. Use any question to move to a point you want to make.

- Keep it simple. Avoid jargon, lingo, and abbreviations. Use language the general public can understand.

- Be articulate. Garbled phrases lead to misunderstandings and misquoting.

- Don't let yourself feel rushed; you can control the pace, but be aware that electronic media is always in a hurry and needs information in "sound bites."

- As a speaker, you know the importance of timing. Use it to your advantage. Use a short but dramatic pause to punctuate your quote, fact, or statement.

- A natural sense of humor goes a long way.

For a phone interview (radio or print journalism):

- Get dressed ready for work. No one but you knows what you have on, but subconsciously if you're ready to "see" and talk to people, you'll perform better.

- Be ready by the phone at the appointed time.

- Have a glass of room temperature water handy, to quickly wash out any "frogs" in your throat. Avoid tapping your fingers, coughing, and other distracting mannerisms.

- Make sure there will be no distractions or interruptions during the interview.

- Arrange to tape the interview. Don't expect the interviewer to send you a copy.

- Have your notes in front of you: large, clear, concise, and READABLE.

- Use notecards instead of paper. You don't want the shuffling noise.

Handling Special Speaking Opportunities

- Have a pencil and paper handy to write down:
  - Name of the interviewer
  - Name of program/column
  - Station call letters/name of publication
  - Location of city where the interview will be heard/appear
- Feel free to stand up. You'll have more energy in your body and therefore project more energy in your voice.
- Be outgoing and spontaneous, but let the interviewer stay in charge.
- If it's a call-in radio show, *listen carefully* to each caller's question. Try to use his or her name in your reply.

For a television interview:

- Wear conservative, business attire in solid colors.
- Avoid black and white. Navy is always great. Bright colors work, but remember that red will dominate everything people see on the screen.
- Avoid noticeable patterns or stripes.
- TV lights can wash you out. If there's a makeup artist on the set, take advantage of this if you can. When applying your own makeup, work to achieve a look that's bright and defined.)
- If you normally wear glasses, wear them.
- Any jewelry needs to be quiet and stay in place.

Speak Up and Stand Out

- No notes. This is the time to be ready with what you want to say. If there's a key point you want to make or crucial information to convey, tell the interviewer. He or she can guide you toward it in the questions that are asked.

- Once you are hooked up to sound (wearing a lavaliere mike or situated close to a boom), assume you are "on." Watch what you say.

- Once you are in the interviewee's chair, assume you are "on camera."

- Focus on the interviewer at all times. Don't look at the camera or members of the crew.

- Sit up straight, no slouching.

- Avoid distracting body language or mannerisms. Only "stars" can get away with preening or fidgeting.

- Use natural gestures as you speak, but watch out for too many. This is speaking in public, but it is not public speaking.

- Let your face show you are enthusiastic about your topic. Smile when appropriate. Look pleasant!

- Relax and enjoy yourself. The audience sees *you* as the expert.

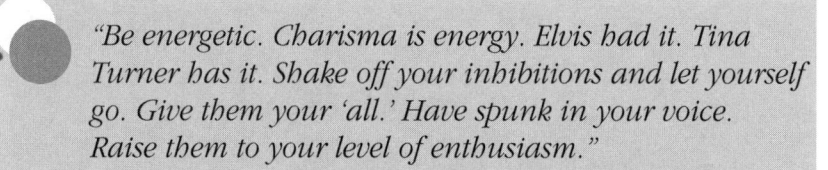

> *"Be energetic. Charisma is energy. Elvis had it. Tina Turner has it. Shake off your inhibitions and let yourself go. Give them your 'all.' Have spunk in your voice. Raise them to your level of enthusiasm."*
>
> —Pam Lontos, speaker/author,
>   *Don't Tell Me It's Impossible Until After I've Already Done It*

Handling Special Speaking Opportunities

twelve

Welcoming Feedback

Q. *Why should I invite criticism?*

A. *Because by listening, you learn.*

As Dr. Norman Vincent Peale put his finger on so deftly, "The trouble with most of us is that we would rather be ruined by praise, than saved by criticism."

Feedback is one of the most important ways for you to improve your public speaking skills, and soliciting it should be a planned, prepared for part of your presentations. Here are some tips to help you create and carry out this important process:

- Use evaluation forms with your audience as often as you can. Watch for recurring comments.

- Audience members will also give you verbal feedback—listen and learn.

- Realize that there are petty people full of agendas, biases, and negativism. To some people, you could never do it right.

- On the other hand, in every group you'll have fans. Soak up their kind words; then, if you really want to improve, ask them casually if they have any suggestions. They loved you, so whatever they say, you can take it!

Speak Up and Stand Out

- After your presentation, gather written evaluations and put them in one of three piles:
    - Very positive
    - Supportive
    - Suggestions for improvement

    Take a good look at the suggestions when you feel strong and want to improve.

- Use the suggestions as indicators of areas you could improve, but be sure you see a trend in the comments before you jump to change. Get rid of those very few evaluation sheets with obviously rude comments, and put them out of your mind.

- Ask trusted colleagues to attend presentations and ask for specific feedback on the area you are trying to improve, such as vocal variety, rephrasing questions from the audience, body language, diction, eye contact, and so on.

- Enroll in a speech class. Part of the classwork will be giving and receiving feedback for improvement.

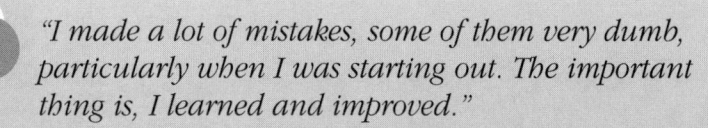

> *"I made a lot of mistakes, some of them very dumb, particularly when I was starting out. The important thing is, I learned and improved."*
>
> —Somers White, professional speaker/consultant

Welcoming Feedback

- Join Toastmasters International, a nonprofit group with clubs all over the world. Members come together in small groups, meeting on a regular basis, and they have a track record for helping people "get the butterflies to fly in formation." The formula for success includes *practice* and *feedback*.

- Another source of help is the National Speakers Association. This is an organization primarily for people who are or who intend to be professional public speakers. There are criteria you must meet in order to become a full member, but you can always attend some meetings as a guest.

- Hire a professional. Even a few sessions with a qualified speech consultant can give you very focused feedback and do wonders for your progress.

Evaluation From Friends and Pros

Create evaluation sheets for anyone you want to give you feedback. Be very specific about what you want your evaluators to look for. The sample included here is appropriate for general use or even for your video run-through.

"People tend to support what they help to create."
—Mona Moon, professional speaker/consultant

Presentation Evaluation Sheet

Title of speech: _____

Name of presenter: _____

Name of evaluator: _____

Date: _____

Mark each statement with an "X" for excellent, "S" for satisfactory, or an "N" for needs improvement.

A. Organization and Development of Content

_____ Opening statement gained immediate attention

_____ Purpose of presentation made clear

_____ Previewed content of speech

_____ Main ideas stated clearly and logically

_____ Organizational pattern easy to follow

_____ Main points supported by examples

_____ Main ideas supported by facts, statistics

_____ Effective use of personal stories

_____ Conclusion well summed up

_____ Audiovisuals clear and visible

_____ AV reinforce and enhance the message

_____ AV use smooth and unruffled

"It takes three weeks to prepare a good impromptu speech."
—Mark Twain

Welcoming Feedback

B. Delivery of Presentation

- _____ Rapport with audience
- _____ Eye contact
- _____ Posture
- _____ Gestures
- _____ Facial expressions
- _____ Movement
- _____ Rate of speech
- _____ Volume
- _____ Voice pitch
- _____ Vocal variety
- _____ Diction

Comments: _____

_____
_____
_____
_____
_____
_____
_____
_____
_____

Evaluation From Your Audience

You will want to draft an evaluation sheet that can give you the kinds of responses you will need to improve as a presenter; that is, it should be easy to understand and easy to fill out. You'll also want to evoke some qualitative comments that might be used, with the participant's permission, as quotes.

Following are some sample evaluation sheet ideas used by many successful speakers. Select the questions that would work best for you. Just remember that whatever format you use, the purpose and value of the exercise is your continuing education.

> *"Here are some dead giveaways of the unprofessional speaker: finds the microphone doesn't work because it wasn't checked out; fumbles and does not start with an aggressive, positive story; and does not come on stage in a positive, powerful way."*
>
> —Dottie Walters, speaker/author,
> *Speak and Grow Rich*

> *"Passion from the platform comes with SPARKLE! Style, Preparation, Action, Real, Komedy, Language, and Emotion."*
>
> —Sheryl Roush, speaker,
> Creative Communication

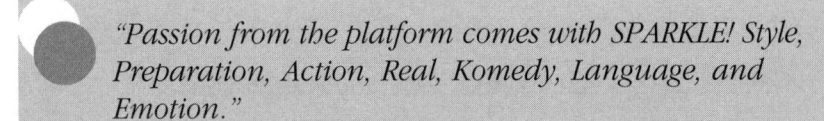

Welcoming Feedback

Participant Evaluation Sheet

What was the most valuable idea you received in the presentation?

_____
_____
_____
_____
_____

What concept(s) will you use immediately?

_____
_____
_____
_____
_____

What do you wish there had been more time for?

_____
_____
_____
_____
_____

May we quote you? Yes____ No____

How valuable did you find the ideas and information?

    1   2   3   4   5
  Low Average Excellent

Speak Up and Stand Out

What did you like best about the speaker's presentation skills?
_____
_____
_____
_____

Do you have any helpful suggestions for improving the presentation?
_____
_____
_____
_____

Optional:

Do you have a friend or business associate who would benefit from this presentation?

Name _____

Address _____

Phone_____

Do you belong to a group looking for a speaker?

Name of group _____

Contact person _____

Phone_____

Welcoming Feedback

Checklists

The Master Plan

One of the most valuable foundation pieces for a successful presentation is a master plan, a step-by-step overview of the process that will serve as both organizer and "laundry list." Following is such a plan, divided into four stages of action. Check items off as you do them. And, of course, take a commonsense approach: you don't have to do the steps in the exact order provided. Make the plan work for *you*.

Stage I: You've Been Asked to Speak

_____ 1. Identify your objectives: inform, motivate, persuade, entertain.

_____ 2. Identify your topic and limit it to a key aspect.

_____ 3. Do a web or cluster chart/mindmap to brainstorm ideas.

_____ 4. Draft an outline of your main points (no details at first).

_____ 5. Write the opener.

_____ 6. Write the closer.

_____ 7. Make a list of the stories, data, and examples you want to be sure to include.

_____ 8. Look at your outline and decide which story, example, or fact does the best job of supporting which point.

_____ 9. Talk through it in a trial run, noting any problems in continuity, logic, or balance. Use a timer. Get a good idea of how much material you have.

_____ 10. Make necessary revisions (change things around, cut or increase your examples, etc.).

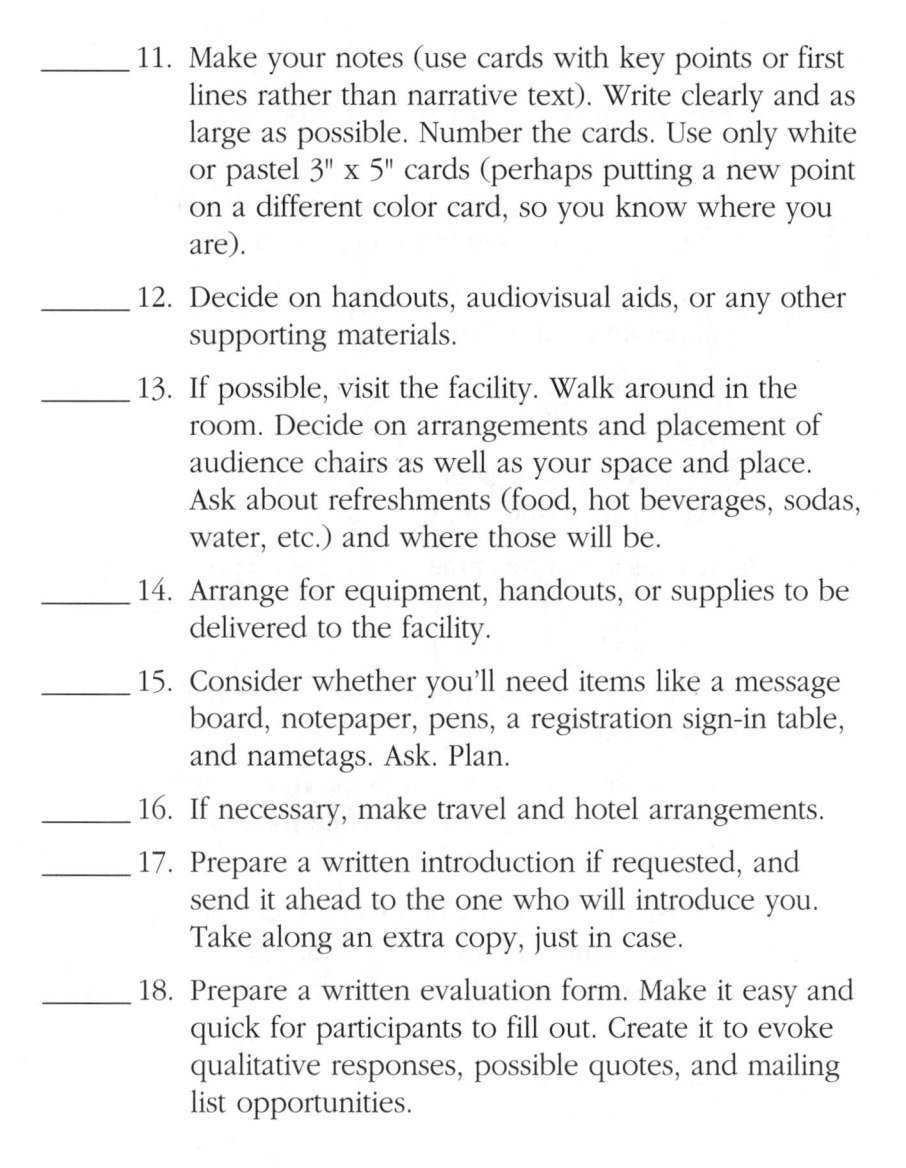

_____ 11. Make your notes (use cards with key points or first lines rather than narrative text). Write clearly and as large as possible. Number the cards. Use only white or pastel 3" x 5" cards (perhaps putting a new point on a different color card, so you know where you are).

_____ 12. Decide on handouts, audiovisual aids, or any other supporting materials.

_____ 13. If possible, visit the facility. Walk around in the room. Decide on arrangements and placement of audience chairs as well as your space and place. Ask about refreshments (food, hot beverages, sodas, water, etc.) and where those will be.

_____ 14. Arrange for equipment, handouts, or supplies to be delivered to the facility.

_____ 15. Consider whether you'll need items like a message board, notepaper, pens, a registration sign-in table, and nametags. Ask. Plan.

_____ 16. If necessary, make travel and hotel arrangements.

_____ 17. Prepare a written introduction if requested, and send it ahead to the one who will introduce you. Take along an extra copy, just in case.

_____ 18. Prepare a written evaluation form. Make it easy and quick for participants to fill out. Create it to evoke qualitative responses, possible quotes, and mailing list opportunities.

Checklists: The Master Plan

Stage II: Time for Rehearsal

_____ 1. Select a time and place where you won't be interrupted.

_____ 2. Warm up your voice. Hummmmm. Sing softly. Read something out loud from the newspaper.

_____ 3. Look at your notes. Find a point you feel excited about and start there.

_____ 4. Now go back over your notes and mentally review each key point, in its proper order.

_____ 5. Talk to yourself. Begin at the beginning of your presentation and talk through it.

_____ 6. Repeat it, but this time looking less and less at your notes. You'll find a natural energy level when you're not attached to your notes.

_____ 7. As you go, review where you'll use certain audiovisuals.

_____ 8. If possible, do a *dry run* in the room you'll be using. If you can't use the same room, then try to find one that's similar.

_____ 9. Consider making a video while you rehearse. Use it for fine-tuning. Turn off the audio to look at your body language and image. Turn off the video: listen to your voice and the content.

_____ 10. Make any changes necessary.

Speak Up and Stand Out

_____ 11. If the presentation or its desired outcome is extremely important, before the big day, give a preview or do a dry run in front of a group. Don't think of this as practice—consider it the actual presentation.

Stage III: The Night Before or Early on the Big Day

_____ 1. Do a final check on the room to make sure it's set up the way you want. Do you have enough chairs and tables? Is the room the right size? Is the physical arrangement appropriate for your group?

_____ 2. Check the audiovisual equipment. Lots of detail must be checked here: plugs, compatible cords, extension cords, cables, spare bulbs, screen, marking pens, and so on. Touch the objects you will use. Get comfortable with the physical setup.

_____ 3. Check the lighting. Decide what lights you want on and know where the switches are.

_____ 4. Check the microphone. Know where the master control is. Test the microphone.

_____ 5. Check all cords that may be running where you or audience members will walk, and have them taped down.

_____ 6. Ask the room setup crew what they can do if you need extra chairs.

_____ 7. Check the room temperature. Ask who will adjust temperature controls, if necessary, as well as where and how that is done. Go with sixty-eight to seventy degrees for most situations. (Too hot is the worst scenario.)

Checklists: The Master Plan

_____ 8. Set up any special displays.

_____ 9. Locate the restrooms and telephones. Inquire about eating facilities nearby.

_____ 10. Take a final look around the room from the audience point of view. Sit in a chair and see what your audience will see. Imagine yourself up there giving a smooth presentation. Then walk out and reenter through the front door as if you were just arriving as a participant. Everything fine? Smile . . . it's coming together.

Stage IV: Tick, Tock . . . Thirty Minutes Before Your Presentation

_____ 1. If you'll be introduced by someone, meet with this person. Have another copy of your intro just in case he or she needs it.

_____ 2. Introduce yourself to the meeting chair, and/or other speakers on the same program.

_____ 3. If possible (and if you haven't done it before, and if there are no audience members present), stand in the spot where you'll start your presentation. Look around and imagine the audience. Walk around. Get comfortable.

_____ 4. Try out the microphone.

_____ 5. Pour a glass of water and set it close by.

_____ 6. Do a final check of audiovisual equipment.

_____ 7. Take a final restroom break and appearance check.

_____ 8. Outside, alone, away from the crowd, take a moment to mentally review the highlights of your presentation. Do your prepresentation ritual: warm up your voice, stretch your body, move around, get the blood flowing. Feel ready to go!

_____ 9. Return to the presentation room and welcome audience members as they arrive. Loosen up and smile!

Checklists: The Master Plan

Bibliography and Suggested Reading

Ailes, Roger. *You Are the Message*. New York: Doubleday, 1989.

Alexander, Roy. *Power Speech: The Quickest Route to Business and Personal Success*. New York: AMACOM, 1986.

Arredondo, Lani. *Present Like a Pro*. McGraw-Hill.

Carlson, Jan. *Moments of Truth*. Cambridge, MA: Ballinger, 1989.

Drummond, Mary-Ellen. *Fearless and Flawless Public Speaking: With Power, Polish and Pizazz*. San Diego, CA: Pfeiffer, 1993.

Fulghum, Robert. *All I Really Need to Know I Learned in Kindergarten: The Essay That Became a Classic*. New York: Villard Books, 1990.

Fulghum, Robert. *Uh-Oh*. New York: Villard Books, 1991.

Huff, Ron. *"I Can See You Naked": A Fearless Guide to Making Great Presentations*. Kansas City, MO: Andrews and McMeel, 1988.

McGraw, Robert. *Learning to Laugh at Work*. Mission, KS: SkillPath Publications, 1995.

McGraw, Nanci. *Organized for Success! 95 Tips for Taking Control of Your Time, Your Space, and Your Life*. Mission, KS: SkillPath Publications, 1995.

Mackay, Harvey. *Swim With the Sharks Without Being Eaten Alive: Outsell, Outmanage, Outmotivate, and Outnegotiate Your Competition*. New York: Ivy Books, 1989.

Molloy, John T. *Dress for Success*. New York: P.H. Wyden, 1975.

Raines, Claire, and Linda Williamson. *Using Visual Aids: A Guide for Effective Presentations*. Menlo Park, CA: Crisp Publications, 1995.

Tannen, Deborah. *You Just Don't Understand: Women & Men in Conversation*. New York: Ballantine, 1991.

Vassallo, Wanda. *Speaking With Confidence: A Guide for Public Speakers*. White Hall, VA: Betterway Publications, 1990.

Wallechinsky, David, and Amy Wallace. *The People's Almanac Presents the Book of Lists #3*. Boston: Little, Brown, 1993.

Walters, Dottie, and Lillet Walters. *Speak and Grow Rich*. Englewood Cliffs, NJ: Prentice-Hall, 1989.

Available From SkillPath Publications

Self-Study Sourcebooks

Climbing the Corporate Ladder: What You Need to Know and Do to Be a Promotable Person *by Barbara Pachter and Marjorie Brody*
Coping With Supervisory Nightmares: 12 Common Nightmares of Leadership and What You Can Do About Them *by Michael and Deborah Singer Dobson*
Defeating Procrastination: 52 Fail-Safe Tips for Keeping Time on Your Side *by Marlene Caroselli, Ed.D.*
Discovering Your Purpose *by Ivy Haley*
Going for the Gold: Winning the Gold Medal for Financial Independence *by Lesley D. Bissett, CFP*
Having Something to Say When You Have to Say Something: The Art of Organizing Your Presentation *by Randy Horn*
Info-Flood: How to Swim in a Sea of Information Without Going Under *by Marlene Caroselli, Ed.D.*
The Innovative Secretary *by Marlene Caroselli, Ed.D.*
Mastering the Art of Communication: Your Keys to Developing a More Effective Personal Style *by Michelle Fairfield Poley*
Obstacle Illusions: Converting Crisis to Opportunity *by Marlene Caroselli, Ed.D.*
Organized for Success! 95 Tips for Taking Control of Your Time, Your Space, and Your Life *by Nanci McGraw*
A Passion to Lead! How to Develop Your Natural Leadership Ability *by Michael Plumstead*
P.E.R.S.U.A.D.E.: Communication Strategies That Move People to Action *by Marlene Caroselli, Ed.D.*
Productivity Power: 250 Great Ideas for Being More Productive *by Jim Temme*
Promoting Yourself: 50 Ways to Increase Your Prestige, Power, and Paycheck *by Marlene Caroselli, Ed.D.*
Proof Positive: How to Find Errors Before They Embarrass You *by Karen L. Anderson*
Risk-Taking: 50 Ways to Turn Risks Into Rewards *by Marlene Caroselli, Ed.D. and David Harris*
Speak Up and Stand Out: How to Make Effective Presentations *by Nanci McGraw*
Stress Control: How You Can Find Relief From Life's Daily Stress *by Steve Bell*
The Technical Writer's Guide *by Robert McGraw*
Total Quality Customer Service: How to Make It Your Way of Life *by Jim Temme*
Twenty-Five Ways to Increase Sales and Profits Without Spending an Extra Dime on Advertising *by Richard Johnson*
Write It Right! A Guide for Clear and Correct Writing *by Richard Andersen and Helene Hinis*
Your Total Communication Image *by Janet Signe Olson, Ph.D.*

Handbooks

The ABC's of Empowered Teams: Building Blocks for Success *by Mark Towers*

Assert Yourself! Developing Power-Packed Communication Skills to Make Your Points Clearly, Confidently, and Persuasively *by Lisa Contini*

Breaking the Ice: How to Improve Your On-the-Spot Communication Skills *by Deborah Shouse*

The Care and Keeping of Customers: A Treasury of Facts, Tips, and Proven Techniques for Keeping Your Customers Coming BACK! *by Roy Lantz*

Challenging Change: Five Steps for Dealing With Change *by Holly DeForest and Mary Steinberg*

Dynamic Delegation: A Manager's Guide for Active Empowerment *by Mark Towers*

Every Woman's Guide to Career Success *by Denise M. Dudley*

Great Openings and Closings: 28 Ways to Launch and Land Your Presentations With Punch, Power, and Pizazz *by Mari Pat Varga*

Grammar? No Problem! *by Dave Davies*

Hiring and Firing: What Every Manager Needs to Know *by Marlene Caroselli, Ed.D. with Laura Wyeth, Ms.Ed.*

How to Be a More Effective Group Communicator: Finding Your Role and Boosting Your Confidence in Group Situations *by Deborah Shouse*

How to Deal With Difficult People *by Paul Friedman*

Learning to Laugh at Work: The Power of Humor in the Workplace *by Robert McGraw*

Making Your Mark: How to Develop a Personal Marketing Plan for Becoming More Visible and More Appreciated at Work *by Deborah Shouse*

Meetings That Work *by Marlene Caroselli, Ed.D.*

The Mentoring Advantage: How to Help Your Career Soar to New Heights *by Pam Grout*

Minding Your Business Manners: Etiquette Tips for Presenting Yourself Professionally in Every Business Situation *by Marjorie Brody and Barbara Pachter*

Misspeller's Guide *by Joel and Ruth Schroeder*

Motivation in the Workplace: How to Motivate Workers to Peak Performance and Productivity *by Barbara Fielder*

NameTags Plus: Games You Can Play When People Don't Know What to Say *by Deborah Shouse*

Networking: How to Creatively Tap Your People Resources *by Colleen Clarke*

New & Improved! 25 Ways to Be More Creative and More Effective *by Pam Grout*

Power Write! A Practical Guide to Words That Work *by Helene Hinis*

The Power of Positivity: Eighty ways to energize your life *by Joel and Ruth Schroeder*

Putting Anger to Work For You *by Ruth and Joel Schroeder*

Reinventing Your Self: 28 Strategies for Coping With Change *by Mark Towers*

Saying "No" to Negativity: How to Manage Negativity in Yourself, Your Boss, and Your Co-Workers *by Zoie Kaye*

The Supervisor's Guide: The Everyday Guide to Coordinating People and Tasks *by Jerry Brown and Denise Dudley, Ph.D.*

Taking Charge: A Personal Guide to Managing Projects and Priorities *by Michal E. Feder*

Treasure Hunt: 10 Stepping Stones to a New and More Confident You! *by Pam Grout*

A Winning Attitude: How to Develop Your Most Important Asset! *by Michelle Fairfield Poley*

For more information, call 1-800-873-7545.

Notes

Notes